MARCO

Tips

JORDAN

TURKEY

CYPRUS   SYRIA

LEBANON

Beirut   Damascus   IRAQ

Mediterranean Sea

Jerusalem   Amman

ISRAEL   SAUDI ARABIA

EGYPT   JORDAN

The best Insider Tips → p. 4

INSIDER TIP

Amman → p. 32

The North → p. 42

The East → p. 50

SYMBOLS

INSIDER TIP   Insider Tip

★   Highlight

●●●●   Best of ...

☼   Scenic view

☺ Responsible travel: fair trade principles and the environment respected

PRICE CATEGORIES HOTELS

Expensive	over 54 JD
Moderate	27 – 54 JD
Budget	under 27 JD

Prices are for a double room per night with breakfast

PRICE CATEGORIES RESTAURANTS

Expensive	over 18 JD
Moderate	6 – 18 JD
Budget	under 6 JD

Prices are for a main meal with non-alcoholic beverage

On the cover: Wall paintings in the desert castle p. 53 | Sailing off the coast of Aquaba p. 80

CONTENTS

The West → p. 56

The King's Highway → p. 64

The South → p. 76

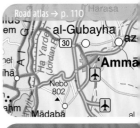
Road atlas → p. 110

DID YOU KNOW?
Timeline → p. 12
Palestinians → p. 21
Local specialities → p. 26
Lawrence of Arabia → p. 38
Books & Films → p. 60
Jean Louis Burckhardt → p. 75
Safe hiking and climbing
→ p. 94
Budgeting → p. 103
Currency converter → p. 104
Weather in Amman → p. 106

MAPS IN THE GUIDEBOOK
(110 A1) Page numbers and
coordinates refer to the road
atlas
(U A1) Coordinates for the
map of Amman in the back
cover. Detailed map of Petra
→ p. 118
The spelling of place names
in the text follows the international phonetic notation
for Arabic

INSIDE BACK COVER:
PULL-OUT MAP →

PULL-OUT MAP 𝄞
(𝄞 A–B 2–3) Refers to the
removable pull-out map
(𝄞 a–b 2–3) Refers to additional inset maps on the
pull-out map

The best MARCO POLO Insider Tips

Our top 15 Insider Tips

INSIDER TIP ▶ Tranquil tea break
The Darat al-Funun in Amman is an enchanted place for art lovers → p. 35

INSIDER TIP ▶ From prison to museum
Once, prisoners languished in Dar Saraya in Irbid. Today, these walls are home to one of Jordan's best-documented and best-kept museums → p. 45

INSIDER TIP ▶ Female power and culinary treats
Fill your picnic basket with home-made delicacies from the Lukmeh Haniyyeh women's cooperative in Irbid and support women's emancipation at the same time → p. 46

INSIDER TIP ▶ Ruler of the oak forest
Fall asleep to the sound of whispering leaves – enjoy romantic overnight accommodation close to nature in a Mediterranean landscape at the Ajloun Forest Lodge stilt constructions with tent roofs → p. 44

INSIDER TIP ▶ Cookies with tradition
Since 1860, the Zalatimo Brothers in Amman have been making the best dry *ma'amul* – delicious biscuits with pistachios, nuts or dates, packed in metal tins, ready to travel → p. 39

INSIDER TIP ▶ Creative paradise
The long-established Balian family paints oriental tiles and ceramic vessels according to your wishes → p. 38

INSIDER TIP ▶ Perfect Friday in Amman
Enjoy fresh fruit juice and home-made cake – during a stroll across the Souk Jara flea market. Discover authentic arts and crafts alongside innovative art projects → p. 89

INSIDER TIP ▶ On the trail of the black iris
In the beautifully located Al Ayoun in northern Jordan you'll find rare plants such as the black iris and accommodation with a local family (photo left) → p. 44

INSIDER TIP ▸ Sunset ahead!

Romantic tour on a historic sailing boat in the Gulf of Aqaba → p. 80

INSIDER TIP ▸ Aperitif in the rock cave

The cosy Cave Bar at the Forum Hotel in Petra has been carved into the rock → p. 74

INSIDER TIP ▸ Gaudy green pleasure

At the Jara Café in Amman the shisha comes accompanied by a fabulous lime-mint cocktail, rounded off with fantastic views of Amman → p. 38

INSIDER TIP ▸ Try the life of the Bedouins

The camp of the Ammarin only a few miles from Petra provides an opportunity to get to know the special way of life of Jordan's first inhabitants at first hand. And not only that: you're doing something for the environment and supporting local Bedouin families → p. 75

INSIDER TIP ▸ Adrenaline rush for adventurous souls

Fabulously varied climbing tour through Wadi Mujib, Jordan's 'Grand Canyon' – with a dip and some abseiling thrown in (photo below) → p. 63

INSIDER TIP ▸ By bike into birders' paradise

Pedalling through primeval marshland in the oasis of Azraq allows visitors to observe rare birds and water buffaloes even, helping the environment at the same time → p. 93

INSIDER TIP ▸ Where the Crusaders ruled over Arabia

Occupying a prominent position on a conical hill since 1115 and visible from afar, much of the monumental Shobak Fort alias Mons Realis (King's Mountain) is unexplored and still awaits restoration. → p. 68

BEST OF ...

FOR FREE

● *Close contact with the rebel poet*

Get on the trail of a rebel against all conventions: in Beit Arar, a historic residence in the Damascene style in Irbid, a free *permanent exhibition* honours the memory of Arar alias Mustafa Wahbi At-Tall, the most important Jordanian poet of the 20th century → p. 45

● *Strolling amongst the ruins*

Clamber around the 2000-year-old *ruins of Pella* to your heart's content, and for free; the surrounding hills have pretty trails waiting to be explored (photo) → p. 58

● *By the light of the silvery moon: open-air cinema*

In the early 20th-century villa of the *Royal Film Commission* on Jabal Amman you can not only watch international films for free, but also get fine shots of the citadel and Old Amman. In the evenings there's open-air cinema under the stars → p. 41

● *Umm al-Jimal – the mother of all camels*

With *Umm al-Jimal* you're visiting one of the most important ancient cities in Jordan and will experience the charm of the everyday in the Roman, Byzantine and early Islamic eras. Admission charge? Nope, it's all free → p. 55

● *Joys of bathing in Aqaba*

You don't have to spend a fortune to sunbathe and swim in Aqaba. At the *well-kept public beach* you'll find everything you need. On Fridays and Saturdays you can also experience Jordanian family life at its best → p. 80

● *Surprisingly green*

In the *Wadi Ibn Hammad* it's as green as in the tropics. And hiking is so easy that you can get by without paying a guide – provided you are not on your own, carry two litres of water and something to cover your head with! → p. 90

●●●● Dots in guidebook refer to 'Best of ...' tips

● *Cookery crash course in Petra*

Would you like to surprise your friends with some Jordanian cuisine after returning, but are not sure whether you have the right recipes? No problem – with Eid Nawafleh in the *Petra Kitchen* restaurant you're allowed to lift the pot lids and a learn few tricks as well → p. 74

● *Frescoes in desert palaces*

Is Islam a killjoy religion? A visit to the desert castles in the eastern part of Jordan might shake up the odd prejudice, as the early Islamic rulers had their baths laid out with *erotic frescoes*, which may be admired at Qasr Amra → p. 53

● *Bedouins with bagpipes*

The red-white keffiyeh on their heads, Scottish bagpipes under their arm, then it's time to blow a tune: a performance of the Royal Jordan army marching band is bound to be a special experience, for instance during the annual *summer festival* held amongst the ruins of Jerash → p. 99

● *Friday is family day*

For Jordanians, family life is the most important part of life: at the weekend, everyone moves to the countryside. Amongst the most popular places for picnics in and around Amman is the *Dibbin Nature Park* near Jerash → p. 49

● *Mosaic art in Madaba*

Artistic enjoyment for the patient: the city of Madaba is famous for its floor mosaics. The replica of the *ancient Biblical map of Palestine* from the St George's Church makes for an excellent photograph → p. 69

● *Wadi Rum – explore the desert with all your senses*

Count the stars at night? Laze by the pool during the day, feel the warm rays of the sun on your face and enjoy the peace and quiet? Or head for the desert on horseback or astride a camel? In the *Bait Ali Camp in Wadi Rum* you can experience the desert in all its aspects. Tahsin and his English wife Susan make it all possible (photo) → p. 85

ONLY IN

BEST OF ...

AND IF IT'S TOO HOT
Activities to brighten your day

● **Balloon trip in Wadi Rum**
40 degrees C (104 °F) in the shade? No problem – take to the air with the *Royal Aero Sportclub* and discover the magnificent landscapes of southern Jordan from above → p. 84

● **Archaeological treasures**
9000-year-old statues take you on an exciting trip back in time – in the pleasantly air-conditioned *Archaeology Museum in Irbid*; English information is provided too → p. 45

● **Water features and sofas in the restaurant**
Cool marble tiles, water features, shade-giving tent roofs and spreading Bedouin sofas on which to stretch out after your meal: the *Reem Al-Bawady* restaurant *in Amman* takes the sting out of 'dog days' → p. 38

● **In the city museum of Jordan's only 'duke'**
Mamduh Bisharat loves old houses. In his *Duke's Diwan,* you're surrounded by numerous images and photographs of an Amman that has long gone. And with a little luck, your host will serve Arabic mocha and traditional sweets → p. 35

● **On top of things in Salt**
In the small town of *Salt,* once seat of government of the emirs of Transjordan, there's nearly always a fresh breeze going. When exploring, don't miss the city museum in the prettily restored Ottoman residential palace → p. 90

● **Oriental dream in Petra**
Not everybody has the wherewithal to overnight at the *Mövenpick Resort Petra*. However, do treat yourself to a drink in the air-conditioned hotel lobby. The interior design and oriental decor of this top-class hotel are overwhelming (photo) → p. 74

HEAT

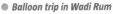

RELAX AND CHILL OUT
Take it easy and spoil yourself

● *Eco trip in Wadi Feynan*

Enjoy vegetarian cuisine and candlelight, far from your mobile phone and internet service – in the Wadi Feynan's *Eco Lodge* you'll find tranquillity. Let your soul run free on the panorama terrace with a 360-degree view across the desert landscape. The solar-powered establishment is amongst the best eco lodges in the world (photo) → p. 62

● *Icy oriental treat*

Melts in your mouth: traditional *mastix ice in a pistachio crust*. Mastix is the resin of the mastix pistachio. Mouth-watering, isn't it! Al-Quds restaurant in Amman is the place to go → p. 36

● *Relaxing on the Dead Sea – for the whole family*

The *Amman Beach* day resort on the Dead Sea boasts a beautiful beach, a large pool and everything else you need to feel good. Children are welcome → p. 63

● *When the sun goes down over Mount Nebo*

Sundown at *Moses' mountain*: the pale-pink evening light lends the contours of the landscape and the ambience a soft hue. A gentle wind caresses the skin, the world appears at peace. Drive there half an hour earlier, to really make the most of this moment → p. 70

● *Relax in the Turkish bath in Petra*

Exploring the extensive red city of rock was incredible, but now the sand scratches in every pore, and your muscles ache – so what could be better than letting yourself be pampered in the *Turkish Bath of the Amra Palace Hotel*? → p. 75

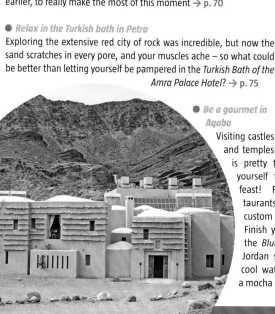

● *Be a gourmet in Aqaba*

Visiting castles and temples is pretty tiring – treat yourself to a culinary feast! Fabulous restaurants await your custom in Aqaba. Finish your dinner in the *Blue Bay* in true Jordan style with ice-cool watermelon and a mocha → p. 79

INTRODUCTION

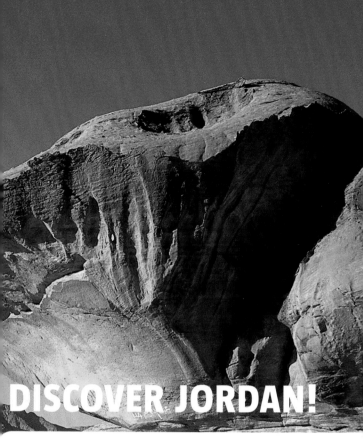

DISCOVER JORDAN!

World history speeded up, imposing natural treasures, fascinating landscapes: the Hashemite kingdom is a small gem – packing in testimonies of the great European and Middle Eastern cultures in a small area. As in a time machine, travellers can trace world history back to its earliest days. The oldest large sculptures in the world, the Ain Ghazzal statues with their expressive faces, seemingly alive – on view at the Archaeological Museum in Amman – created by artists in the 8th millennium BC. The highlight of any trip to Jordan is the rock city of Petra, which the Nabataeans carved into the reddish rock from the 6th century BC onwards. Greeks, Romans, Christians, Muslims and Crusaders all left their impressive marks on the territory that today is the Kingdom of Jordan.

Yet the country not only lends itself to a stroll through history, it also boasts stunning natural treasures. This region at the interface of the Mediterranean and the great desert of the Arabian Peninsula has some spectacular scenery. In the south you have the desert of Wadi Rum with its fine sand and wonderful red rocks jutting

Photo: Quarry in Wadi Rum

Mediterranean scenery: olive groves are a common sight in the north of Jordan

into the skies. This is the most beautiful part of desert areas which make up 90 per cent of Jordan and which have marked the population and their identity. The vastness and loneliness of this landscape reduces everything down to the core: simple gestures, no superfluous words, controlled emotions. These qualities have emerged over thousands of years where the people adapted to their hostile surroundings. The Jordanians' unassuming, near-reticent politeness has its origins here. But they are also characterised by a down-to-earth philosophy of life: Ramadan is not marked with fairs and festivities late into the night or people milling around in the street after breaking the fast. Jordanians celebrate within the circle of their family, in their own house.

Only a few miles from Wadi Rum the Red Sea awaits, a paradise for divers with its coral reefs and fish-rich waters. In contrast, the Jordan Valley, where a subtropical climate supports the cultivation of vegetables, unfolds green and more green, as far as

the eye can see. At its southern point the Jordan flows into the Dead Sea, which at 400m/1300ft below sea level marks the lowest point on earth. With its high salt and mineral content it has been a destination for health tourism since time immemorial. And in the north you'll find a Mediterranean hilly landscape with olive groves.

Despite Jordan's many attractions, for a long time the country was not exactly in the spotlight of the travelling world. The explanation for this is the political situation in the region. The image of this buffer state between Israel/Palestine and Iraq is affected by the unstable conditions in its neighbouring countries. However, Jordan itself – even after the terror attacks on hotels in Amman in 2005 – remains a safe country to travel in, both in a regional and a global context. Not for nothing did the World Economy Forum of Davos choose Jordan as the stage for its special meetings in the region.

Tourists are treated like royalty. People are friendly and helpful, yet they never pester. With the possible exception of Petra you will not have a horde of souvenir sellers pursuing you or children asking for money. Taxi drivers work by their functioning taximeters, dispensing with the need for tiresome haggling over the fare. Thanks to the good educational system, many Jordanians speak English. Road signage is always bilingual: Arabic and English. This makes Jordan an ideal destination for independent travellers who prefer to go and discover it on their own.

> **Many Jordanians speak English**

1812
The Swiss orientalist Jean Louis Burckhardt discovers the rock city of Petra

1900–1908
Construction of the Hejaz Railway

1920
Britain is given a mandate by the League of Nations for Transjordania, Palestine and Iraq

1921
Emir Abdullah becomes the provisional ruler of Transjordania, his brother Faisal King of Iraq

1946
Jordan gains independence, Emir Abdullah is crowned king

Today's Jordan is a relatively recent state, established under British colonial rule. The idea was to create a kingdom for their ally Abdullah: Transjordan, as the territory under British mandate was known at the time. The 'small king' Hussein, grandson of the founder of the state Abdullah I, was adept at creating a role for his country far beyond its geographical size. After Hussein's death in 1999, his son Abdullah II stepped up to the succession. With his beautiful Palestinian Queen Rania at his side, Abdullah II is a popular guest in the West. In terms of the economy, he has brought in young technocrats to walk the corridors of power. However, there have been few political reforms.

> **King Abdullah II is a welcome guest in the West**

Yet Jordan could do with some of those. The around 6.5 million inhabitants of the country are on average 22 years old. The rapid increase in population is not without problems – many young people can't find work and are forced to emigrate. There is also a strong contrast between rich and poor, and no middle class to speak of. In the high-class quarter of Abdoun in western Amman, it's all palatial residences, with at least two cars in the garage, where domestic staff are employed to do the housework. Despite unemployment, there are certain tasks that Jordanians will not accept. The gardeners in the fine residential districts and in the Jordan Valley, for example, are usually Egyptians. Due to the conservative code of honour of the Bedouin and Islam, Jordanian women will not work in a stranger's household. Being on their own in the house with a man would compromise them. This work is taken on by women from the Philippines, Sri Lanka and Bangladesh.

> **Many young people can't find a job and leave the country**

In the eastern part of Amman, in contrast, one room is usually shared by a whole family; the houses are concrete buildings standing close to one another, and often just bare concrete. Yet there's little downright misery, and you won't see any slums. This is thanks to foreign aid intended to stabilise Jordan in this volatile region and to

1948
Foundation of Israel. Hundreds of thousands of Palestinians flee across the Jordan. Jordan occupies the West Ban and East Jerusalem (annexation in 1950)

1953
Hussein becomes King of Jordan

1967
Jordan loses the West Bank and East Jerusalem to Israel in the Six Day War, but retains administrative powers until 1988

1970/71
The Jordanian army puts down a revolt by the Palestinian organisation PLO (Black September)

The contrast between rich and poor dominates Jordanian society – there is no substantial middle class

guarantee the pro-western stance of the royal family, but also thanks to remittances sent by Jordanians living abroad.

The Jordanians still trust the leadership qualities of King Abdullah II, but even traditionally royalist groupings are calling for change, measures against corruption and more social justice. Environmental campaigners are mobilising protests against the introduction of nuclear power and the exploitation of non-renewable water reserves. However, deep political change or violent regime change are not on the cards. Jordan remains a fascinating and at the same time safe destination in an otherwise rather restless region.

If you take the trouble to pick up a few phrases in Arabic, Jordanians' doors and hearts will open even wider. Many are pleasantly surprised to see western visitors taking an interest in their language and culture. Don't just discover the historical sights of Jordan, dive into the contemporary Arabic universe too. *Ahlan wa Sahlan* – a warm welcome.

1994 Peace treaty with Israel

1999 After the death of King Hussein, his oldest son is crowned King Abdullah II

2003 The invasion of Iraq led by the USA leads to the immigration of hundreds of thousands of Iraqis to Jordan

2010 Parliamentary elections: conservative parties win

2011 Army officers loyal to the monarchy and tribal leaders demonstrate on the streets for the first time, demanding reforms

WHAT'S HOT

1 Arty

Arabian Art Amman's *Orfali Art Gallery (Kufa Street 46)* provides a proper showcase for Jordanian artists. The *Dar Al-Anda Art Gallery (Dhirar Bin Al-azwar Street),* too, looks after promoting home-grown talent. Here you can still make true discoveries – and there are concerts and readings too. A very promising representative of the art scene is Rima Mallah, whose works can be purchased in Amman from *Love on a bike (Rainbow Street, photo above).*

Upwardly mobile 2

Canyoning Explore spectacular gorges with the canyoning guides of *Terhaal (48 Ali Nasuh Al Tahir Street, Amman, www.terhaal.com, photo centre)* and secured by a rope. One of the destinations in the canyoning programme run by *Lizard Life (www.lizard-life.com)* are the waterfalls of Wadi Himara. And those pros behind *Jordan Tracks (www.jordantracks.com)* know the basalt and sandstone gorges along the Dead Sea like the back of their own hand .

Jabal Amman

3

Capital gem The alleys of Jabal Amman are full of young people strolling amongst boutiques, bars and restaurants. Rainbow Street with its many coffee places und shops in particular is worth a visit. Take a break at *La Calle (1st Circle, www.brande nite.com/lacalle-jordan).* The roof terrace affords an excellent view across the city. Near the 3rd Circle, capital dwellers party till morning at *Kanabaye* where live bands join alternating DJs. The sound has a rockier vibe at *Amigos (1st Circle).*

Jordan on the move

Walking fever Everything started with the *Amman Fastwalk* group on facebook. Now nearly the whole country has been caught by the walking fever. Over a hundred people meet for the Fastwalk evenings run by Mowaffaq Maraqa, which take a fleet-of-foot crowd on changing routes through Amman. Even the *Royal Society for the Conservation of Nature* has joined the trend, developing the *Jabal Amman Walking Trail*, which leads from Jabal Amman to Jabal Luweibdeh. The starting point is at the *Wild Jordan Centre (www.rscn.org.jo, photo above),* where you can also pick up a trail map. *Responsible Travel (www.responsibletravel.com)* organises hikes through Jordan's most beautiful landscapes, amongst them a trek around the popular Wadi Rum or on the *Al Ayoun Trail* in the north of the country.

Desert dining

Traditionally prepared Would you like to sample authentic Jordan cuisine? At the *Darna Village* hotel restaurant *(South Beach Road, Aqaba, www.darna-village-aqaba-jordan-hotel.com, photo below)* you may also witness a traditional style of preparation whereby the ingredients are cooked for hours in the sand. At *Beit Sitti (6 Mohammad Ali Al Sa'di Street, Amman, www.beitsittijo.com)* guests take matters into their own hands and prepare a typical four-course meal themselves. The result is eaten together in this atmospheric house in the Weibdeh neighbourhood. A Bedouin tour is another way to see what's cooking in Jordanian pots and pans *(www.bedouinroads.com).*

IN A NUTSHELL

BEDOUIN

A proud and freedom-loving people that cross the sandy seas of the desert with their camels: the culture of the Bedouin (Bedu, to be precise) is omnipresent in Jordan. In truth, the ancestors of King Abdullah II weren't Bedu, but settled merchants in Mecca. The high estimation that the Bedouin way of life enjoys in Jordan is grounded in the fact that the Bedu are loyal to the Hashemite ruling dynasty. Nearly all Bedu in Jordan today are settled, many working in tourism. Travellers who want to hear from the horse's mouth how the Bedu experience the balancing act between tradition and modernity will appreciate the moving book Married to a Bedouin by Marguerite van Gel-dermalsen. In 1978 New Zealand-born Marguerite married a Bedouin from Petra and for the first ten years of their marriage shared a cave with him in the rock city.

COFFEE

In Jordan, coffee, qahwa in Arabic, is not just a beverage, but a way of life. The Bedouins celebrate the roasting and boiling of the green coffee as a ceremonial ritual to express appreciation of the guest. The bitter, aromatic hot coffee is taken in tiny sips – three times in a row at the most. The fourth cup should be refused. Most Jordanians don't think of Bedouin ceremonies when they think coffee, but rather of a black mocha. After waking up, to greet a visitor or after

Photo: Modern headscarves

A society on the move – in Jordan, modern life and the past come together in a unique way

a good meal – a little cup will always be served, according to individual taste *sada* (without sugar), *chafiif* (with little sugar) or *masbuut* (medium sweet). The mocha tastes differently in Jordan because the coffee powder *(bunn)* is boiled in an long-handled pot *(Ibrik)* up to seven times, and because the coffee is left to rest for a few minutes before draining, to make sure the dregs don't settle on the tongue. Jordanian mocha is often flavoured with cardamom *(heel)* or cinnamon *('Irfe)*.

GENDER

Even though most women wear a headscarf: Jordan has no official separation of genders, nor is the wearing of a headscarf enforced. And in terms of education, Jordanian women are at the top in the Arabic world. Still, the day-to-day life of women and girls is marked by patriarchal laws and ways of thinking. Most Jordanian parents still prefer sons to daughters to preserve the family name. This means that in most cases the family is only considered complete

women don't play much of a role. Since 2003, they have at least been entitled to 5 per cent of all seats in the national parliament, thanks to a quota. At municipal elections, women achieve a quota of 20 per cent.

MOTORBIKES

For many years, foreign motorbikers had the country's numerous beautiful panoramic roads nearly to themselves: only tourists, the police and His Majesty King Abdullah II himself were allowed to ride a motorbike in Jordan. In the future, regular Jordanian citizens will also be allowed to give it all they've got on their bikes in their own country. In Naur, halfway between Amman and the Dead Sea, the Royal Motorcycle Club of Jordan, founded in 2008, has opened a modern training centre for aspiring bikers. Apart from offering courses, the club will also at least provisionally be in charge of issuing licenses. The club also sees its role as a go-to agency and information point for tourists who would like to travel Jordan on their own motorbikes. The homepage provides information on current motorbiking events in the country. *Royal Motorcycle Club | www.rmcj.jo*

NABATAEANS

The Nabataeans were a mysterious Bedouin tribe whose dominion at the height of their power stretched from Damascus all the way to the Sinai. Settling in the kingdom of Edom, which today is southern Jordan, in the 6th century BC they dominated the trade routes of the old Arabian world for centuries. During the rule of the Roman Emperor Augustus the Nabataeans are said to have transported 10,000 camel loads (or 1.5 t) of incense to Rome in a single year. For centuries, this pacific and egalitarian

Much more than just a beverage for Jordanians: coffee

when the woman has borne at least two sons. In Jordan, legal status is dependent on religion. While the Islamic law system (sharia) may be interpreted in a progressive fashion, the conservative interpretation usually applied in Jordan puts women at a disadvantage. In terms of inheritance law and the right to custody of their children, Jordanian women have a harder time: divorce is more difficult to demand, and they have to accept up to three other wives. In politics,

society successfully defended its position amongst the great powers of the region. The city of Petra was one of the most cosmopolitan places in the world of the time, bringing together Greek, Egyptian and Semitic artistic influences. Petra enjoyed fame for its architecture and the sophisticated canal system that supplied it with water. In AD 106, the territory of the Nabataeans was absorbed into the Roman Empire, Petra becoming the capital of the Roman province of Arabica. The caravan routes migrated to Palmyra (in today's Syria), triggering the Nabataeans' decline. Several earthquakes (in AD 365 and AD 746) caused Petra to be abandoned by its inhabitants. The city of rock fell into oblivion, and was only rediscovered in 1812 by the Swiss researcher Jean Louis Burckhardt.

POLITICS

King Abdullah II's western style and promises of reform may give the impression that Jordan is on the way towards political democratisation. However, the king enjoys a unique degree of power – being the de facto head of both the executive and the legislative. Gerrymandered constituencies ensure that representatives of loyal tribes dominate parliament. The members of the second chamber, the senate, are hand-picked by the king. He is also head of the armed forces and selects the judges. Most of the media are in the hands of the state. There is no freedom of the press. While political parties have been allowed since 1992, they are subject to strict state control. In politics, women play a very minor role indeed. However, there are legal quotas in the parliament (5 per cent) and in the municipal councils (20 per cent) for them. In 2007, a woman was elected mayor for the first time without benefiting from the quota.

RELIGION

97 per cent of the Jordanian population are Sunni Muslims. The only Shiites can be found amongst Iraqi immigrants, who however don't enjoy Jordanian citizenship. About 2 per cent of the population are Christians. Thanks to their loyalty towards the monarchy and the royal family's religious tolerance they enjoy a prominent position in economy and politics.

PALESTINIANS

The foundation of the state of Israel in 1948 completely destabilised the young Jordanian state. Some 350,000 Palestinians fled their homeland for the neighbouring country. Today, the percentage of Jordanians with Palestinian heritage is estimated to be just under half the country's 7 million inhabitants, but there are no official statistics: the issue is a political hot potato and is often swept under the carpet. For a long time, Israeli politicians declared that Palestinians didn't really need their own state, as they already had one in Jordan. What is true is that Palestinians are better integrated in Jordan than in the other Arab states: they enjoy Jordanian citizenship and dominate the economic life of the country. However, they are still denied high positions in the army or state.

In contrast to other countries in the region there has never been a Jewish community in Jordan. The Hashemite royal family traces its family tree back to the prophet Mohammed who received the wait-born computer expert who married into the family from abroad is probably better known than her husband Abdullah II. Photographs of this elegant lady, who has a penchant for Italian couture,

Most Jordanians are Sunni Muslims: daily life at the Al-Hussein Mosque in Amman

Holy Scripture, the Koran, by revelation. In Jordanian laws however, Islam plays hardly any role, with the exception of marital and family law, which as in all Arabic countries is grounded in religion.

ROYAL FAMILY

Tracing its history back to the prophet Mohammed, the Jordanian royal family *(www.kingAbdullah.jo)* for centuries administered the holy sites of Mecca and Medina. This gives them the status of one of the noblest families in the Arabic Islamic world. In the west, Queen Rania *(www.queenrania.jo)*, a Ku-

fill many pages of the society magazines. She married Abdullah II in 1993. Apart from supporting social projects and women's rights in Jordan, Queen Rania also sits on the board of the World Economic Forum of Davos. The couple have four children.

While the royal couple with their modern appearance are popular in the West, in their own country they haven't been able to emulate the degree of popularity enjoyed by King Hussein and Queen Noor, the last and popular wife of King Hussein. While Abdullah II at the beginning of his rule mingled incognito amongst his people to experience the work of authorities or hospitals, many Jordanians miss the down-to-earth style that characterised his father.

SHISHA AND COOL JAZZ

When Omar Abdallat warbles 'Ha shemi, Hashemi', nobody in Jordan is in any way surprised – local artists are expected to proffer eulogies for the king and the military. Those who enjoy something more romantic prefer pop stars from neighbouring Arabic countries: Ilham Al-Madfai and Kazim As-Saher from Iraq, Abdullah Ruweished from Kuwait, Amr Diab from Egypt or Syria's Asala are favourites. Otherwise there is a small 'alternative' music scene in Jordan too, whose exponents take their cue from global trends. In the trendy clubs of Amman the shisha pipes are lit to the tunes of Cool Jazz: fusion guitarist Kamal Musallam, who is now based in Dubai, recorded half a dozen CDs and collaborates with names like Billy Cobham. The jazz cover band Sign of Thyme and the rock band Jadal put in regular appearances in clubs and at festivals. The female singers Macadi Nahas and Shireen Abu Khader (Dozan Ensemble) present classy arrangements of traditional Arab folklore. With his laconically performed ballads, rock musician Yazan Rousan has his very own style. For those wanting to take some music back home with them: Arabic original CDs in good quality are stocked at the Amman Virgin Store (City Mall) or at Books@Café, and are also of course available through the internet (look out for the labels OrangeRed and Inkognito).

WASTA

Wasta is the Middle East version of the 'old school tie' or other helpful 'connections'. Relatives or acquaintances are used to secure a position in the civil service or a place at university, sort out a problem with the authorities or pull in a business commission. This social practice was born from the traditional system of values: loyalty towards the tribe or the extended family is greater than that towards the state and nations. However, this system blocks social mobility: often it is not performance that determines employment, but family influence. This frustrates many well-qualified young people who prefer to emigrate to the Gulf States or the West. Access to important political office is also restricted to a limited number of families. Abdullah II has broken up this pattern in part, bringing in young business and IT professionals with a proven track record to work with him. Still, *wasta* continues to be a foundation of Jordanian society.

WATER

Jordan is amongst the ten most water-deprived countries in the world. 90 per cent of the country is desert. While daily water consumption at an average 83 litres per head is one of the lowest in the region – in Israel for example, it stands at 275 litres per head – fast population growth will bring Jordan a gigantic water deficit by the year 2020. Today already, the water tanks atop houses are only filled once a week. In the summer there are regular water shortages. The government has been investing in the water sector for years, building dams to collect rainwater and improving the water and wastewater management. Still, price politics favour agriculture, which uses up the lion's share of available water, yet only contributes 3.5 per cent to Jordan's gross domestic product. Pumping off non-renewable water reservoirs is leading to salinification and other environmental damage.

FOOD & DRINK

Despite all invocations, the Arab world has not achieved political unity. However, gastronomically, the countries of the region have a lot in common.

For Jordan this means you'll find the classic Levantine cuisine which emerged from Lebanon and Syria. It's main element are the famous cold and warm starters, *mezze*. This choice of salads, vegetable dips, cheese and chunks of meat is served in the centre of the table in small bowls, with everybody helping themselves. This underlines the social character of food, which in Jordan often brings together the entire extended family. Pita bread forms a core element of every meal and is used like a spoon: use a piece of bread to scoop up some food and to place into your mouth. Al-

ternatively use the long rigid salad leaves called *khass* for dipping. At home people will often eat together from bowls. However, whether during a private dinner or at the restaurant, you may of course also place a portion on your own plate. Travellers are often surprised to see the table groaning under the various starters. As the *mezze* are not only delicious but also quite filling, you might prefer to order just starters and decide afterwards whether you actually want to order a main dish to follow. Doing it this way makes particular sense for vegetarians, as in Jordan the main dish usually consists of grilled meat with side orders. Fresh fish is available in Aqaba; otherwise it is mostly imported frozen from Yemen or Saudi Arabia.

Photo: *Mezze* – the traditional starters

Culinary temptations – the famous *mezze* for starters, followed by grilled meat as the epitome of a good meal

Funds permitting, the Arab world enjoys eating meat, and a good quantity of it. This holds true for Jordanians too. For most, *brosted*, a crispy fried chicken, or *dalu*, a chunk of braised mutton, fulfils the criteria for a good meal. However, the varied Levantine cuisine also offers a large selection of tasty meat-free dishes: *hummus*, fried falafel balls, small dough pouches filled with spinach, cheese or *zaatar* (a thyme-like herb mix), stuffed vine leaves, parsley-bulghur salad, crunchy fried *halloumi* cheese and grilled

vegetables – all these palate teasers are standard even in average Jordanian restaurants, as is *tahina* – an aromatic sauce from sesame paste, water and lemon – or *shanklish*, a fresh cheese made from dried yoghurt which is then mixed with various herbs and spices.

If you have the chance, do try the Jordanian national dish: *mansaf*. This is a Bedouin dish that you won't find in any other Arab country, and it is truly unique: think of a mountain of rice, with the various parts of a sheep distributed liberally

LOCAL SPECIALITIES

DISHES

▶ **aurak einab** – vine leaves, filled with rice and/or mincemeat and spices
▶ **baba ghanush** – puree made from grilled aubergines
▶ **baklawa** – several layers of dough, with chopped nuts and honey syrup
▶ **falafel** – small fried vegetable balls in flat bread with salad (photo left)
▶ **ferach meshwi** – half a chicken, grilled
▶ **ful** – large brown beans with garlic, olive oil and lemon juice
▶ **hummus** – chickpea dip with sesame oil and lemon juice
▶ **kibda** – small pieces of grilled chicken liver
▶ **knafeh** – a favourite dessert! Mozzarella-like fine white cheese oven-baked with very thin vermicelli noodles and sweetened with sugared water. Ask for a portion without the sugared water.
▶ **kofta** – mincemeat balls
▶ **kubba (kibbe)** – meatballs made from burgul (cooked dried wheat) with a pine-nut filling
▶ **kusa mahshi** – courgettes filled with rice

▶ **ma'amul** – dry pastries with nuts or dates
▶ **mohallabiya** – milk pudding with rose or orange-flower water
▶ **mutabbal** – aubergine puree with sesame oil and yoghurt cream (photo right)
▶ **sambusak** – small puff- pastries, filled with mincemeat, cheese or spinach
▶ **shawarma** – Arab version of doner kebab, made with mutton
▶ **shish kebab** – barbecued mincemeat skewers
▶ **shish taouk** – grilled chicken pieces on a skewer
▶ **shorbat ´adas** – pureed yellow lentil soup flavoured with cumin, served with croutons and lemon
▶ **tabuleh** – bulghur wheat salad with onions, tomato and a lot of parsley

DRINKS

▶ **assir burtuqal** – freshly squeezed orange juice
▶ **assir lamun** – fresh lime juice
▶ **qahwa masbut** – Turkish coffee
▶ **shay** – tea with a lot of sugar and on request with fresh mint (shay bil na'ana'a)

over it. The rice is saturated with a camel yoghurt sauce. After being dried, this yoghurt sauce is then sold in the shops in balls the size of a tennis ball. It liquefies again when water is added, lending the rice a distinctive, often quite strong taste. Recommended drinks are freshly squeezed fruit juices (e.g. orange, lime) and mineral water. Alternatively, try a mild drinking yoghurt called *laban*. Sadly, in many restaurants you'll only find a choice of western soft drinks such as Fanta or Coca Cola. The usual drink of choice after a meal is tea with fresh mint or coffee. Alcohol is available in most hotels and European restaurants. However, some western restaurants don't actually serve alcohol. If you would like a glass of wine with your meal, it's a good idea to always ask straight away whether the restaurant serves alcohol or not. During the fasting month of Ramadan this is only the case in the large hotels. Light and refreshing Amstel-brand beer is produced under licence in Jordan. There is also imported canned beer.

Local wines come from the area around the heavily Christian-influenced town of Madaba; the red INSIDER TIP Saint George is particularly recommended. The quality of the other wines, including those imported from Israel and Palestine is middling. However, if you see a Lebanese wine from the estates of Kefraya or Ksara on the wine list, go for it. These wines are excellent, even if – like all imported goods in Jordan – they are expensive too.

To make up for this, are all kinds of delicious sweets can be found on the menu in Jordan: honey-sweet and calorie-laden to a fault, whether *knafe*, a flat hot mozzarella with roasted vermicelli noodles and syrup, or *busa arabiya*, a delicious mastix vanilla ice-cream coated in pistachio. Mastix is the aromatic heart of the pistachio tree. Last not least, *attaif* are small crêpes filled with nuts or a kind of ricotta. Although they are a Ramadan speciality really, Amman's Old Town has the baker Abu Ali, who makes them all year round.

A popular drink in Jordan: hot freshly brewed tea

SHOPPING

On your flight to Jordan leave some space in the suitcase for the way home. Clothes, shoes, home fabrics and souvenirs are readily available here, at good prices. Bath salts, masks and creams with active ingredients from the Dead Sea make very popular little gifts. Amman and the duty-free zone of Aqaba are paradise for shoppers. However, don't bother with the shopping mall when in Aqaba, as practically all they sell is mass-produced in China. In Amman you'll find cheaper alternatives to the expensive malls on Jabal Hussein (Duwar Firas). If you're in the mood to bargain, start at about a third of the asking price. Some shops will issue a tax-free form as proof of your purchases. A minimum spend of approx. 60 JD entitles you to get VAT back at the airport when you leave the country.

CARPETS

The village of Mukawir, about half-an-hour's drive from Madaba, is where the INSIDER TIP only truly Jordanian carpets are made. The women from the Bani Hamida tribe weave carpets from sheep's wool in vivid red, turquoise and green using traditional looms. However, the design of these objects, up to 2 by 3 metres in size, is rather clunky and a world away from the simple elegance of traditional Bedouin textiles.

CRAFTS FROM JORDAN'S NEIGHBOURS

Many of the souvenirs for sale in Jordan are from the neighbouring countries. Syria, for instance, produces INSIDER TIP small wooden boxes with marquetry work (from 5 JD) and hand-engraved round brass trays (tabaq), mostly bearing Arabic lettering or animals and flowers: the small ones are good for serving at table, the others as a side table (in Amman-Weibdeh, at Paris Square and from Al-Afghani). Syria also exports richly embroidered cotton tablecloths in many colours and sizes. Most of the decorative domestic pottery (approx. 4 JD for a snack bowl, approx. 18 JD for a salad bowl) on sale in Jordan is made in the Palestinian Territories (Hebron and Jerusalem). It is no coincidence that the flower and animal motifs of the pretty mugs, wall plates and cake platters in strong tones of blue, white, red, pink, brown and green are similar to those produced in Kytachia in Turkey. It was

Colourful sand bottles, culinary delicacies and Arab art – Jordan boasts a choice of original souvenirs

from there that immigrants brought the craft and designs to Palestine at the end of the 19th century.

MUSIC, LITERATURE, ART

The biggest selection of Arab CDs and books in Amman is available from the City Mall and – on a slightly more modest scale – the Mecca Mall. Books@Café too is fairly well stocked. The CDs and DVDs sold in the city centre are a lot cheaper, however, as nearly all are pirated copies. If you would like to buy modern Arab art, head for the Orfali Gallery in Umm Utheina or the Dar Al Anda gallery (near Darat Al-Funun, Jabal Weibdeh).

SAND BOTTLES & MOSAIC ART

Due to the lack of a medieval urban culture and the artisan tradition that goes with it, there is very little in the way of authentic crafts. Colourfully filled sand bottles – usually with camel or oasis motifs, but also with abstract designs on request – make an original present. One highlight is mosaic art from Madaba, created by graduates of the college for restorers, who produce wall plates and mirror frames following ancient animal and plant motifs.

SPICES & HERBS

Delicious souvenirs to nibble that are only available in this form in Jordan include fresh spices from the market, date biscuits *(mamul bi-tamr)* or freshly roasted mixed nuts and kernels (in Amman from *Safeways*, for instance, or slightly more expensive at the airport). Another typically Jordanian-Palestinian speciality is the thyme-sesame-sumak herbal mix called INSIDER TIP ▶ *zaatar*. Stirred in with good-quality olive oil, this is delicious with salads, on pizza or with sheep's cheese.

THE PERFECT ROUTE

FROM THE CAPITAL INTO THE WILD EAST

First of all, get your bearings, gaining an overview of ❶ *Amman* → p. 32 from Cita-del Hill. After a detour to the Archaeological Museum you will learn to appreciate the steps on your way to the Roman Theatre. Then head east across the city past Sports City and get on the N 30. The following desert drive ends in the ❷ *Azraq wetlands reserve* → p. 51. Stay overnight at the Azraq Lodge and take a hire bike to Azraq Castle.

THE MOST BEAUTIFUL DESERT CASTLES

After a guided bike tour into the nature reserve in the morn-ing, get onto the N 40 heading for the 'top two' desert cas-tles, ❸ *Qasr Amra* → p. 53 with its erotic wall paintings and the majestic ❹ *Qasr al-Kharana* → p. 54. Back in Amman explore the quiet Jabal Weibdeh neighbourhood and let the day come to a tranquil end with a non-alcoholic nightcap on the terrace of the Rakwat Arab café.

THE LOVELY NORTH

Heading north, the well-maintained road leads across green hills and the Zarqa River. From the King Talal Dam it's not far to the fork in the road leading to ❺ *Jerash* → p. 47 (photo l.). After visiting the spec-tacular ancient ruins of the town, have a meal at the Lebanese House Umm Khalil or head straight into nearby ❻ *Ajloun* → p. 42 and climb the imposing Crusader castle. A good accommodation option is the Ajloun Forest Lodge, before driving to the university town of ❼ *Irbid* → p. 45 to visit the Archaeological Museum and the municipal museum of Saraya.

THREE-COUNTRY VIEWPOINT

In ❽ *Umm Qais* → p. 46, the Gadara of antiquity a good 30-minute drive away, take your time exploring the ruins of the town and the excavation sites. Refuel at the Rest House with a view of Lake Tiberias (Sea of Galilee) and the point where three countries come meet: Jordan/Syria/Israel.

DOWN TO THE LOWEST POINT ON EARTH

Trundle down into the Jordan Valley amidst gorgeous almond and olive tree plantations. Why not enjoy your afternoon coffee at the Rest House of ❾ *Pella* → p. 58? The 2000-year-old ruins of the ancient city lie on a green slope and offer a

wonderful opportunity to stretch your legs before continuing to the Dead Sea. At **10** *Amman Beach* → p. 63 you can find out what it feels like to float suspended in the salt water.

GLIMPSE OF THE PROMISED LAND

From the Dead Sea, it's not far to **11** *Mount Nebo* → p. 70. You should aim to get there an hour before sunset, to give you time to visit the basilica and take in the overwhelming landscape. On the country road it'll take about 20 minutes to reach **12** *Madaba* → p. 68, where you can admire the ancient mosaic map of Palestine at St George's Church.

THROUGH THE DESERT AND ON TO THE RED SEA

On the King's Highway south you'll pass **13** *Wadi Mujib* → p. 63, perfect for climbing tours and canyoning. Back on track, head for **14** *Karak* → p. 67 with its famous Crusader castle. The road is lined by ruins up to the point where a detour leads to the **15** *Dana* → p. 64 nature reserve (photo r.), which provides excellent hiking. Further south at Wadi Musa you reach the famous city of **16** *Petra* → p. 71. Make sure you have plenty of time to explore this fabulous city of sandstone. 788 steps lead up to Ed Deir with its stunning views. The Desert Highway then takes you on to **17** *Wadi Rum* → p. 83 where you can sleep under the stars in the Bedouin camp or drive on to the country's southernmost tip at **18** *Aqaba* → p. 77. This is the place to dive down to the colourful coral reefs of the Red Sea.

Approx. 980km/610mi.
Driving time only: approx. 20 hours
Recommended travel time: 14 days
Detailed map of the route in the road atlas, the pull-out map and on the back cover

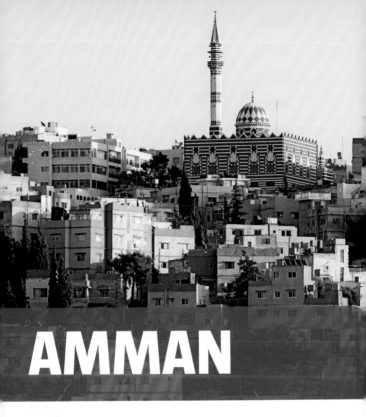

AMMAN

MAP INSIDE BACK COVER
(112 C5) (*⚄ D5*) **Arriving by plane, Amman marks the starting point for a round-trip through Jordan.**

Amman (pop. 2.5 million) is one of the most modern and cleanest capitals of the region. The houses are clad in light or reddish limestone, lending the city a uniform appearance. Up to now, there are relatively few high-rises. Instead the city, originally laid out on seven hills, spreads out in all directions, now covering some twenty hills (*jabal*).

The Citadel is a good vantage point for following the development of the city: one of the main traffic arteries, Zahran Street, leads from the 1st Circle, a roundabout, to the 8th Circle. The historical city centre with administration buildings and banks lies in the valley below the 1st Circle. From here, the city has expanded west to Wadi as-Sir beyond the 8th Circle. Any route description uses these two roundabouts as references.

At first glance, it might be hard to believe that Amman is amongst the world's oldest cities. Apart from monuments from antiquity and a few traces of the Islamic Middle Ages, the oldest houses only date back to the 1920s. At that time, the small settlement of Amman on the eponymous river became the unofficial capital of Transjordan. However, the first traces of human settlement go all the way back to the 8th millennium BC. Around 1200 BC, Rabbath-Ammon was the capital of the Empire of the Ammonites, which is the origin of the current name. The settle-

Photo: View of Amman and the Abu Darwish Mosque

Traditional and modern – one of the world's oldest cities, Jordan's capital Amman also boasts first-class restaurants and cafés

ment became more widely known in the 3rd century BC under the rule of Ptolemy II, when it was called Philadelphia.

Amman has very significant and well-preserved archaeological sites. However, the tourist and the general urban infrastructure are still at a low level of development. In the run-up to 2015 though, a makeover of the Old Town is planned. A number of problems could be solved with relatively little financial effort. For instance there's a lack of public elevators to access the neighbourhoods situated high-

---

CITY WHERE TO START?
Citadel Hill *(Jabal Al Qalaa)* **(U E6)** *(ᗕ e6)*. From here you have the best view of the Roman theatre and the Old Town. Flag down one of the yellow taxis – public buses often only have Arabic lettering. Car parks are few and far between, so you're better off leaving the hire car in the hotel garage.

er up. The streets are full of taxis, and the exhaust fumes from the heavy traffic tend to hang around between the many hills. For visitors, the taxis are handy of course – taking a bus with no knowledge of Arabic

AL-CHECK HUSSEIN MOSQUE (U E6) *(ᛗ e6)*

Only built in the 1920s, by Emir Abdullah, the mosque with its two elegant minarets is the symbol of the Old Town.

Colossal size: columns of the Hercules Temple on Citadel Hill

can turn into a bit of an adventure and is not really recommended. Taxis are hailed by hand signal. The Balqa region around Amman boasts many attractive destinations for a day trip: Wadi Sir for instance, Fuheis and the royal city of Salt (see chapter Tours & Trips).

SIGHTSEEING

ABDULLAH MOSQUE (U C4) *(ᛗ c4)*
The city's largest mosque was erected in 1989 in honour of the first ruler of modern Jordan. Inside, women have to wear a cloak *(abaja)*. *Sat–Thu 8–11am | admission incl. museum 2 JD, Abaja 1 JD | Abdali*

The Jordanians have a special reverence for this mosque because the second caliph, Omar ibn al-Khatib (634–44), had already built a mosque here. Independent travellers may only view it from the outside. *Al-Hashimi Street*

ARCHAEOLOGICAL MUSEUM ★ (U E5) *(ᛗ e5)*
The small museum at the far end of the Citadel area shows exhibits from 10,000 years of history. Right at the entrance a display case houses some statues from Ain Ghazzal, examples of the oldest large anthropomorphic sculptures in the world, dating back to the 8th mil-

lennium BC. The statues were found by chance during construction work for a motorway outside Amman; their faces seem incredibly alive. *For opening times and admission see Citadel*

INSIDER TIP ▶ DARAT AL-FUNUN 〰
(U E5) (*m e5*)

The 'little house of the arts' is a true oasis in Amman. Consisting of several historic buildings, the complex consists of an exhibition room, a mainly English-language media library and a pretty garden. The small café, accessible via a set of steps, offers wonderful views. At the fountain, sometimes a musician will get out a lute and play an impromptu concert. *Sat–Thu 10am–7pm | free admission | Jabal Weibdeh, Nimer bin Adwan Street | www.daratalfunun.org*

DUKE'S DIWAN ●
(U E5) (*m e5*)

A meeting place for artists, with an warm welcome for everybody in a building dating from 1924. Free coffee. If host Mamdouh Bisharat is there, he serves *knafe*, hot cheese with sweet vermicelli. The walls of the seven rooms are adorned with many images and photographs of Amman from the first half of the 20th century, books, and sometimes exhibitions. *April–Oct Sat–Thu 10am–6pm, Nov–March Sat–Thu 10am–5pm | free admission | King Faysal Street 12*

JABAL AL-QALAA (CITADEL) ★ 〰
(U E5) (*m e5*)

The Citadel hill offers a nice view across the Old Town with its Roman theatre. At sundown Amman is bathed in a soft light. From up here you also get to watch a Jordanian national sport: pigeon training. In the early evening, hundreds of pigeons circle above the town before returning to their dovecotes on the roofs.

The area consists mainly of fields of ruins dating from various eras. To the left of the entrance lie the remains of the Temple of Hercules built in the 2nd century AD under Marcus Aurelius. Now, only a few colossal columns recall the former size of the edifice. You'll find the most impressive building behind the small museum at the far end of a field of ruins: the imposing entrance to the 7th-century Umayyad Palace. This restored monument is the only part of the palace to withstand an earthquake shortly after the building's completion in 749. *Admission April–Oct daily 8am–6pm, Nov–March daily 8am–4pm | visits April–Oct daily 8am–7pm, Nov–March Sat–Thu 8am–5pm, Fri 9am–5pm | admission 2 JD (incl. Archaeological Museum) | guided tour in English 15 JD per hour*

JORDAN MUSEUM (U D6) (*m d6*)

Several thousands of square metres of exhibition space, around 2000 historical finds from all parts of the country: the

---

★ Archaeological Museum
The enchanting Ain-Ghazzal statues from the 8th millennium BC have features that seem positively alive → p. 34

★ Jabal al-Qalaa (Citadel)
Umayyad Palace and Roman ruins in lofty heights → p. 35

★ National Gallery
The modern face of Arabic art → p. 36

★ Roman Theatre
Excellently preserved example of Roman architecture from the 2nd century → p. 36

MARCO POLO HIGHLIGHTS

Jordan Museum tells the story of the area covered by the Jordanian state from the Palaeolithic up to the present day. In collaboration with partner institutions from all over the world, ambitious contemporary exhibitions are planned too. When this edition was going to print, according to the museum's management the opening was imminent. For English-language information on opening times and ticket prices check *www.jordanmuseum.jo/en. Ras Al Ain | tel. 06 4 62 93 17 and 06 4 61 16 47*

INSIDER TIP ► **ROYAL AUTOMOBILE MUSEUM** (112 C5) (*∅ D5*)
The recent history of Jordan is retraced in an exhibition hall by means of the cars of the country's rulers. Alongside a few limousines owned by the founder of the state, Abdullah I, visitors can mainly view the state limousines and sports cars of 'little King' Hussein, who ruled the country for over 40 years. The historic photos and short videos show the monarch visiting the Circassian Guard, at the races in the *Rumman Hill Climb* and at his return from the USA after a last cancer treatment shortly before his death in 1999. King Abdullah II can be seen as a child on small-scale replica sports cars. *Sat–Mon, Wed 10am–5pm, Fri 10am–7pm | admission 3 JD | King Hussein Park, exit off King Abdullah II. Street (formerly Medical City Street), leading from the 8th Circle in the direction of Irbid | www.royalautomobilemuseum.jo*

NATIONAL GALLERY ★ (U C5) (*∅ c5*)
The museum is laid out around a sculpture park with a children's playground and Japanese garden. On view are modern Arab art and works by western artists inspired by the region. *Sat–Mon, Wed 9am–7pm, Fri 10am–5pm | admission 5 JD | Jabal Weibdeh | www.nationalgallery.org*

NYMPHAEUM (U E6) (*∅ e6*)
The splendid fountain west of the Roman theatre was erected at the end of the 2nd century. Today, all that remains is a monumental rock wall which used to form the rear of the fountain. *Behind the Al Hussein Mosque*

ROMAN THEATRE ★ (U F5) (*∅ f5*)
Very well preserved and restored theatre in the centre of Amman's Old Town, constructed in the 2nd century AD on the flanks of the Al-Taj hill. The theatre held 6000 spectators. In summer visitors can experience its good acoustics at concerts. *Sat–Thu 8.30am–7pm, Fri 10am–4pm | admission 1JD including Folklore Museum and Museum of Popular Traditions | Al-Hashimi Street*

RESIDENTIAL QUARTER (U E6) (*∅ e6*)
Stroll through Jordan's more recent history in this neighbourhood dating from the 1930s *(see Tour no. 2)*. Lying at the end of Rainbow Street, heading off east from the 1st Circle, this is where the political elite of the British protectorate of Transjordan built their houses, and is also the site of the birthplace of King Hussein. *Jabal Amman*

FOOD & DRINK

AL-QUDS (JERUSALEM) RESTAURANT (U E5) (*∅ e5*)
Simple, traditional Arabic fare and excellent sweets, amongst them ● mastix ice cream in a pistachio crust. A true institution in Amman for both locals and tourists. *Daily | Old Town, at the beginning of King Hussein Street | tel. 06 4 63 01 68 | Budget*

INSIDER TIP ► **ASH-SHARQ** (U E6) (*∅ e6*)
Bring your own fish, and the chef de cuisine will prepare it the way you like it, for instance baked in *bagdunsiya*, a sauce

with sesame paste and parsley. Before that, tasty starters and ice-cold draught beer are served on the terrace. Coming from Faisal Street opposite Hashim's Restaurant in the Wahmanat passage (left-hand alley); choose your dinner in the fish shop to the right and pay, then head up the stairs to the left at the end of the passage. *Daily | tel. 06 4 63 01 68 | Moderate*

INSIDER TIP ► BOOKS@CAFÉ ☺
(U E6) *(∭ e6)*

Bookshop with internet terminals selling second-hand travel reading in various European languages. The first floor has a ☼ café-restaurant with a large terrace and far-reaching views. *Daily | Omar Bin al-Khattab Street 12 (off Rainbow Street) | tel. 06 4 65 04 57 | www.booksatcafe. com | Moderate*

CAFÉ WILD JORDAN ☼ ☺
(U E6) *(∭ e6)*

Restaurant with fabulous views of the Old Town and Citadel, healthy and imaginative non-alcoholic fruit cocktails. Architect Ammar Khammash placed one of the city's most modern buildings in one of the oldest neighbourhoods. The offices of the Royal Society for the Conservation of Nature (RSCN) and a shop with the Society's merchandise are headquartered here too. *Mon–Sun | Osman bin Affan Street, off Rainbow Street | tel. 06 4 63 35 42 | www.wildjordancafe-jo. com | Moderate*

FAKHR ED-DIN
(U D5) *(∭ d5)*

Best Arab restaurant in Amman (Lebanese cuisine), housed in an elegant restored 1950s villa with garden. *Daily | Taha Hussein Street | 1st Circle, behind the Iraq embassy | tel. 06 4 65 23 99 | Moderate–Expensive*

JAFRA CAFÉ **(U E5)** *(∭ e5)*

The latest gossip, accompanied by mocha and *shisha*; there are readings and other cultural events too. *Daily | Downtown, broad house entrance opposite the post office, 1st floor | tel. 06 4 62 25 51 | Budget–Moderate*

Coffee, second-hand books, internet access – books@café makes travellers happy

JARA CAFÉ ❧
(U D6) (𝄞 d6)
Café-restaurant for nearly any time of day, featuring an extensive terrace, cosy seating and great views of Jabal Weibdeh. Non-alcoholic cocktails. Follow the sign diagonally across from the British Council a few steps downhill. *Daily | Rainbow Street | tel. 079 5078033 | Moderate*

MUHTARAF AL RIMAL ❧
(U E5) (𝄞 e5)
On the edge of the Weibdeh neighbourhood, painter Abdelaziz Abu Ghazaleh has converted a former school diagonally opposite the Firas Hotel (down the steps through the yellow garden gate) into an atelier-cum-open-air-café. Ideal for coffee, *shisha* and updating your travel diary – unless there's a film team using the historical backdrop. *Daily | Nimr Al Adwan Street tel. 06 4624140 | Budget*

REEM AL-BAWADY ●
(112) (𝄞 D5)
Arab dishes served at round tables in huge rooms with traditional decor. Water features, tents and Bedouin sofas. Popular with groups of tourists, but also with local families. *Daily | Tla'al-Ali-Viertel, Mohamed al-Fayad Street | tel. 06 5515419 and tel. 06 5512030 | Budget–Moderate*

SHOPPING

AL-BURGAN FOR HANDICRAFT
(U C5) (𝄞 c5)
Embroidered tablecloths, fabrics, linenware and furniture, some of it antique, are for sale in this family-run concern behind the Hotel Intercontinental. *12 Tala't Harb Street, 2nd Circle, Jabal Amman | www.alburgan.com*

OLD TOWN
(U E–F5–6) (𝄞 e–f5–6)
Apart from a small gold market there are the usual souvenirs such as water pipes, musical instruments and leather bags.

BALIAN CERAMICS
(U E6) (𝄞 e6)
In 1920, the Armenian Balian family brought Ottoman ceramic art to Jerusalem. In the Amman branch you can purchase items like door signs and drinking cups and have them personalised as well.

LAWRENCE OF ARABIA

These days, the adventurer Thomas Edward Lawrence (1888–1935), better known as Lawrence of Arabia, is nearly forgotten in Jordan. That may have to do with the fact that in his autobiography Seven Pillars of Wisdom, he doesn't describe the Hashemite dynasty in the most flattering terms. However, in the West, the legend lives on. As a British liaison officer, the Oxford-educated oriental scholar, soldier, archaeologist and writer joined the army of Faisal, later King of Iraq, whose father Sherif Hussein had proclaimed the revolt against the Turks in World War I. Lawrence helped the Arab tribes to cooperate and go on to fight a guerrilla war. Their first great victory was the taking of Aqaba in 1917. The Arabs however felt betrayed when they didn't receive the great empire the British had promised.

Rainbow Street 8, Jabal Amman | www.armenianceramics.com

JORDAN RIVER FOUNDATION ☺
(U E6) (*⑪ e6*)

Woven carpets, embroidered tablecloths, crafts and cosmetics are for sale in the sales rooms of this foundation with workshops all over the country. *Com-*

INSIDER TIP ZALATIMO BROTHERS
(U D4) (*⑪ d4*)

The Zalatimo family make the best biscuits in town, at two branches. Their palate ticklers come packed in decorative metal tins, ready for travelling. *Abdali, Jawharat Al-Quds Building | Shmeisani, Abdel Hamid Sharaf Street | www.zalatimo.com*

Cool shopping in the air-conditioned City Mall

ing from the 1st Circle, left off Rainbow Street | www.jordanriver.jo

SHOPPING MALLS

The modern air-conditioned shopping centres offer international designer brands and fashion chains. For the biggest selection of international branded stores, head for the *City Mall (opposite King Hussein Park, not far from the 8th Circle)* (112 C5) (*⑪ D5*). For nearly the same level of choice and a more central location go to the *Taj Mall (Abdoun)* (U A6) (*⑪ a6*), which opened in late 2011. *www.citymall.jo*

SPORTS & LEISURE

JOGGING (U C2) (*⑪ c2*)

Those who don't like running on asphalt may prefer the INSIDER TIP *jogging trail in Sports City* (opposite the basketball hall), which was laid out under pine trees. Turn right off Al-Malakah Alia Street at the corner of the Royal Cultural Center, make an about-turn after 300 m and use the entrance on the right-hand side. *Harun al-Rashid Street | free admission*

TURKISH BATHS (U E6) (🗺 e6)

Sheer relaxation after a walk round the city: the *Al-Pasha* traditional Turkish baths have a steam bath and sauna. Allow yourself to be scrubbed down with a loofah sponge, and stick your legs into a basin of cold water, while sipping hibiscus juice. Massages can also be arranged. You'll need to book – and to

CINEMA

Cinemas usually show Hollywood productions and Egyptian comedies (English or Arabic with subtitles). For current programmes see *www.jordancinemas.com. Galleria at the Abdoun Circle* (U A6) (🗺 a6) | *Centurys in the Zara Center behind the Hyatt Hotel on the 3rd Circle* (U C5) (🗺 c5) | *Grand*

Oriental alleyways and bazaars? None of that in the modern capital of Amman

bring swimming togs. There are different times for women, men and mixed groups. *Mahmud Taha Street, branches off Rainbow Street | tel. 06 4 63 30 02 | admission 25 JD*

ENTERTAINMENT

ABDOUN CIRCLE (U A6) (🗺 a6)

On this roundabout in the residential quarter of Abdoun, upper-class youth come to party. *Tche-Tche* has hookahs in all flavours, while the gloomy *Irish Pub* serves a wide choice of beer. The *Planet Hollywood Cafe* has an American vibe. Very pretty is the *Blue Fig Cafe* with its location on the slope of the hill behind the Abdoun Circle, where regular live concerts are held too. At *Flow* near the Taj Mall, international DJs animate on Thursdays and Fridays.

Theatres in the *Mecca Mall | Mecca Street* (112 C5) (🗺 D5)

THEATRE AND CONCERTS

For information see *www.jordantimes.com.* Events are held in foreign cultural institutions or in private arts centres such as the *Al Balad Theatre (Jabal Amman)* (U E5) (🗺 e5) and 🌿 *Makan (Weibdeh)* (U E5) (🗺 e5), also at the *Royal Cultural Center (Shmeisani, Al-Malika Alia Street | tel. 06 5 66 10 26) | www.rcc.gov.jo* (U B2–3) (🗺 b2–3) and the *Al Hussein Cultural Center (Ras Al Ain)* (U D6) (🗺 d6).

INSIDER TIP ► VINAIGRETTE 🌿
(U B3) (🗺 b3)

Restaurant and club. Super sushi, top views of the city. *Shmeisani, side entrance of the Al-Qasr Metropole Hotel | reserva-*

tions required | tel. 06 56 20 52 83 21 |
Budget–Moderate

INSIDERTIP CANARY HOTEL
(U D5) (*m d5*)

Quiet, basic, hotel in Weibdeh with family atmosphere. Child-friendly terrace. Single to five-bed rooms with bath, telephone, TV, fan, tiled floors. Internet in the common room. Handy location on the Old Town–Weibdeh Park service taxi line (back of the Terra Santa College). *20 rooms | Karmaly Street | tel. 06 4 63 83 62 | canary_h@hotmail.com | Budget*

FARAH HOTEL (U E5) (*m e5*)

For backpackers: ventilator in the room, shared bathroom, Bedouin tent, friendly atmosphere. *24 rooms | Cinema Al-Hussein Street | tel. 06 4 65 14 43 and 4 65 14 38 | www.farahhotel.com.jo | Budget*

HISHAM HOTEL (U B5) (*m b5*)

The rooms could really do with a lick of paint, but the cosy ambience, garden terrace and central location make guests come back time and again. *25 rooms | Mithqal al-Fayez Street, 3rd Circle | tel. 06 4 64 63 27 | www.hishamhotel.com.jo | Moderate*

INTERCONTINENTAL (U C5) (*m c5*)

The classic amongst the five-star establishments, a meeting place for politicians, diplomats and journalists. Outstanding service. *478 rooms | Zahran Street, between 2nd and 3rd Circle | tel. 06 4 64 13 61 | www.amman.intercontinental.com | Expensive*

JORDAN TOWER HOTEL (U F5) (*m f5*)

Good-value hotel under friendly management right by the Roman theatre. Tiled floors, free Wi-Fi, bookable on the internet. *17 rooms | 06 4 61 41 61 | Hashemiya Street 48 | www.jordantoweramman.com | Budget–Moderate*

JORDAN TOURISM BOARD
(U A5) (*m a5*)

Tunis Street, between 4th and 5th Circle | Call Center tel. 06 5 00 80 81 | www.visit-jordan.com

LOW BUDGET

▶ The guesthouse of the Theodor Schneller School 😊, a good 10km/6mi northeast of Amman *(next to the Marka Camp)* offers an excellent alternative accommodation. Children can play in the green recreation spaces, on the playground and in the rope garden. The school uses the profits generated to support the education of young boys from underprivileged families. (Early) reservations required. *20 rooms | tel. 05 3 61 61 03 | www.ems-online.org*

▶ Tourists like to browse Amman's biggest second-hand market. Alongside clothes, you can buy inexpensive edible souvenirs, e.g. spices, herbs or fine-grained wheat bulgur. *Abdali Square* (U C–D4) (*m c-d4*)

▶ The ● Royal Film Commission resides in an early 20th-century villa on Jabal Amman. Its offerings include an international film programme, in the evening also open-air cinema. *Mango Street 5 | tel. 06 4 64 22 66 | free admission | www.film.jo* (U E6) (*f e6*)

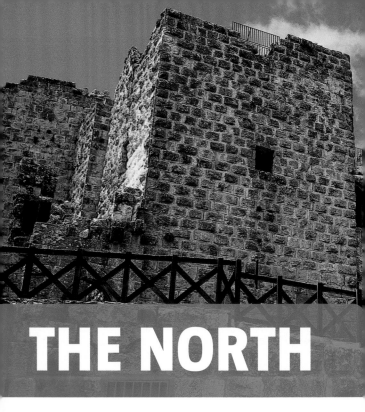

THE NORTH

Jordan is greenest up in the hilly north. Up to 600mm/24in of precipitation falls each year around Ajloun, Irbid and Umm Qais, and in winter it may even snow in this Mediterranean-looking landscape.

In spring you wander over the hills though a sea of colourful meadow flowers. Olive and almond trees, even some forests of oak and pines, lend welcome shade. Back in Antiquity this water-rich area was very sought-after – evidence of which can be seen in the numerous remains of important Roman cities, most of all Gerasa (Jerash) and Gadara (Umm Qais). The imposing fort of Ajloun is a reminder of conflicts with medieval Crusaders.

AJLOUN

(112 B3) *(CD C4)* **25km/15mi northwest of Jerash, the centre of Ajloun (pop. 20,000) features an old mosque with an elegant minaret.**

What Ajloun is most famous for, however, is its castle, on the top of a mountain outside the town.

SIGHTSEEING

QALA'AT AR-RABAD ★ ☆

The imposing fortress of Qala'at ar-Rabad above the small town of Ajloun can be seen from afar. Built by a general and nephew of the Arab military commander Salah ed-Din in 1184/85, it is

Photo: The Qala'at ar-Rabad fortress at Ajloun

Encounters with world history in the north of Jordan – in a famous Roman city and a medieval Muslim fortress

one of the most beautiful examples of Islamic military architecture in the Middle East. Despite its near-unassailable position, the Mongols stormed and plundered the castle in 1260. The Mamluks made the fort part of a chain of castles and posts, allowing them to send news by light signal or courier pigeon from Cairo to Damascus or Baghdad within twelve hours. *Sun–Thu 8am–6pm, Fri 8am–5pm | admission 1 JD | visitor centre tel. 02 6 42 0115*

FOOD & DRINK

AL-JABAL RESTAURANT ☆

Enjoy fabulous views of the castle and the soft surrounding hills from the spacious shaded terrace. In the afternoon in particular the interplay of colours between sandy rocks, green Aleppo pines and steel-blue sky is stunning. Inside, the friendly owners have kitted out the restaurant very cosily with wooden furniture and warm colours – this place is a good choice both when it's boiling hot and in

Irbid is a university town and the administrative centre of the north

cool wintry weather. Simple, tasty Arab food and international cuisine. *Daily | Ajloun-Jordan Al Qala'ah Street | tel. 02 6 42 20 22 or 02 6 42 09 91 | www.jabal-hotel.com | Moderate*

WHERE TO STAY

INSIDER TIP ▶ AJLOUN FOREST LODGE 😊

The most original choice of accommodation is the Forest Lodge run by the Royal Society for the Conservation of Nature. You sleep in rustic stilt buildings with tent roofs or comfortable wooden bungalows under oaks and Aleppo pines. Generous Jordanian breakfast with local produce. Hiking tours take you to Arabic calligraphers, biscuit bakers and soap producers, some of them allowing visitors to watch the production. Sometimes you might even be able to try your own hand at the task. To get there, take a left 5km/3mi beyond Ajloun on the way to Irbid and look for signs to the *Ajloun Nature Reserve.* 10 *cottages with up to 3 beds (April–Oct), 5 chalets with max. three beds (all year round) | tel. 02 6 47 56 73 or via the RSCN in Amman, tel. 06 4 61 65 23 | www.rscn.org.jo (Wild Jordan/Ajloun Forest Reserve) | Moderate*

INSIDER TIP ▶ GUEST ROOMS AND CAMPSITE IN AL AYOUN

The asphalted country road leads you to the community of Al Ayoun (a good 17km/10mi north) set in beautiful scenery with fine hiking trails, caves and climbing spots (more information in the 2011 hiking guide *Al Ayoun Jordan* by Tony Howard and Di Taylor). The inhabitants of Al Ayoun, Rasoun and Orjan offer guest rooms with breakfast and/or full board, as well as tent accommodation. The accommodation is basic, but good value. *8 rooms (not all in the same place), 4 tents in Rasoun Camp, sleeping 2–4 people each | reservations tel. 077 2 21 96 04 |www.rasouncamp.com |* Moderate

AL-JABAL CASTLE ☄

Basic hotel with en-suite rooms. Some of the balconies have a view of the fortress. *20 rooms | Al-Qalaa Street | tel. 02 6 42 02 02, tel. 02 6 42 09 91 | www.jabal-hotel.com |* Moderate

IRBID

(112 C2) (ᗯ D3) With its 500,000 inhabitants the city is the administrative centre of the north.

The many cafés and snack bars near Yarmouk University are busy till midnight.

MUSEUM FOR ARCHAEOLOGY AND ANTHROPOLOGY ●

The museum is considered the best of its kind in Jordan. Highlights include the 9000-year-old statues from Ain Ghazal, one of the earliest settlements of humankind. Coming from Amman turn left at the sports stadium roundabout, then after 500m/550yd right around the stadium. After another 500m/550yd you'll see a sign to your left. The staff at the gate can help. *Sun–Thu 10am–1.45pm and 3–4.30pm | free admission | Institute of Anthropology & Archaeology, Yarmouk University | www.yu.edu.jo*

BEIT ARAR ●

Historic residence in the Damascene style opposite the Irbid Municipality/Baladiya: the rooms are grouped around a courtyard with stone cobbles. Photos and documents tell the story of Arar alias Mustafa Wahbi At-Tall, Jordan's most significant 20th-century poet. *Daily 8am–3pm | free admission | tel. 079 9 05 54 62 (director Samir Ibrahim)*

INSIDER TIP ► DAR SARAYA

The picturesque 19th-century building opposite the Municipality/Baladiya was once the residence of the Ottoman governors. Later on, it housed a prison. And since 1994, the palace has been home to a permanent exhibition on the history of Irbid. The house is kept very well, the exhibition is carefully documented, incl. in English. Don't miss the room with mosaics from Roman times. The courtyard is used for arts events. *April–Oct daily 8am–6pm, Nov–March daily 9am–5pm | free admission*

AL-HARAM CAFÉ

Popular meeting point for students and young travellers – with a pyramid-shaped glass roof. *Daily | University Street |* Budget

---

★ **Qala'at ar-Rabad**
The fortress of Ajloun – this is where the Arabs put up a valiant fight against the Crusaders
→ p. 42

★ **Umm Qais (Gadara)**
Enjoy fantastic views all the way to Israel and Syria across the remains of the once-mighty ancient city → p. 46

★ **Jerash**
One of the best-preserved Roman cities in the world and once the economic centre of the Provincia Arabica → p. 47

MARCO POLO HIGHLIGHTS

IRBID

INSIDER TIP ▶ **LUKMEH HANIYYEH (DELICIOUS BITE)** ☺

Feast at the *Microfund for Women project*: alongside Jordanian classics such as *maqlube* (rice with fried cauliflower or

Umm Qais: the ruins of the ancient city of Gadara, situated on a hilltop

aubergine) and *maftul*, there are homemade starters and desserts to choose from, also as take-away options. Coming from Amman, turn off at the fourth traffic light, then keep right. *Daily | tel. 079 9 67 16 11 and 077 5 48 79 59 | Rateb Al Batayna Street, opposite the Plateen pharmacy | Moderate*

MANGO RESTAURANT AND CAFÉ

Clean, nicely furnished, tasty food and good value into the bargain. Choose between sandwiches, oven-baked cutlets with fries and salad, fruit juices and cappuccino. Right next door the Mango baker magicks up aniseed crescents and ginger cookies. Popular with students, and suitable for groups too. *Daily | tel. 02 7 27 25 28 | University Street (Shafeeq Irsheidat Street) | Budget*

NEWS CAFE

Pretty location for an espresso or a convivial evening: milkshakes, pizza, shisha – and lots and lots of young people. *Daily | At the Al-Joude Hotel | Budget*

WHERE TO STAY

HOTEL AFAMIA

Small quiet mid-range hotel, a bit outside the centre. Light-filled, clean rooms with tiled floors and air-conditioning, TV and minibar. Receptionist Muhammad can help if you're having trouble finding the hotel. *20 rooms | King Abdullah Street, opposite the electricity company | tel. 02 7 10 18 66 | www.aphamiahotel.com | Budget–Moderate*

AL-JOUDE HOTEL

Near the mosque in the university quarter. *15 rooms | tel. 02 7 27 55 15 | joude@ go.com.jo | Moderate*

WHERE TO GO

UMM QAIS (GADARA) ★ ☼
(112 B2) (*∅ C3*)

Don't miss taking a trip to the place where three countries meet, some 30km/18mi away, in the furthest northwest of Jordan. The heights supporting the ruins of the town of Umm Qais give you a fantastic view: of the Golan Heights in Syria, across Lake Gethsemane into Israel and the Jordan Valley. At the foot of an Ottoman settlement, discover the ruins of ancient Gadara. Probably founded around 300 BC by the Greeks, Gadara would later become one of the most important cities of the Decapolis, with the arteries of ancient commerce going north leading past here. The extent of the ruins gives an impression of how powerful Gadara must once have been. Note the impressive *theatre* of black basalt stone, which used to hold 3000 spectators. Another stunning monument is actually underground: a few years ago, archaeologists discovered Antiquity's longest underground aqueduct. Make sure to take a break at the ☼ INSIDER TIP *Resthouse* restaurant *(daily | tel. 02 7 50 05 55 | www.romero-jordan.com | Moderate)* within the ruins complex *(daily 8am–6pm | admission 4 JD | museum Wed–Mon 8am–5pm | free admission | tourist police tel. 02 7 50 01 34)* – the view from the terrace onto the Golan Heights and Lake Gethsemane is unique. Good Arab cuisine too.

JERASH

(112 C3) (∅ D4) ★ **The ruins of Jerash, ancient Gerasa, are considered the best-preserved Roman settlement in the world. As a Jordanian tourist attraction, they are only topped by Petra.**

At just a bit over 50km/30mi north of Amman, the ruins are easily visited as part of a day trip from the capital. Built from orange-pink limestone, Gerasa used to lie on one of the most important trading routes of Antiquity. There is no consensus on whether Gerasa was founded by Alexander the Great or one of his generals. However, the Hellenistic city had its heyday under Roman rule in the 2nd and 3rd centuries, when it belonged to the association of cities that made up the Decapolis.

A visit by Emperor Hadrian in AD 129 led to a major construction boom, turning the city into the economic heart of the Provincia Arabica. It was also on the new Via Romana, a paved road connecting Aqaba with Damascus. In its heyday 20,000 people lived in Gerasa. It was under Byzantine rule that decline set in, and the city was abandoned by its last inhabitants in the 9th century. Every summer though it is brought back to life, with both theatres staging operas and concerts.

SIGHTSEEING

The sights are presented in the sequence of the usual circular walk around the complex *(if no other information is given: April–Sept daily 8am–6pm, Oct–March daily 8am–4.30pm | visitor centre at the southern gate | tel. 02 6 35 12 72 | admission 10 JD)*.

LOW BUDGET

▶ A quasi-Tuscan feast: amidst a beautiful Mediterranean landscape, the ☼ *Lebanese House Umm Khalil* in Jerash **(112 C3) (∅ D4)** serves excellent Levantine cuisine at very reasonable prices. Highlight: the large outside terrace. *Jerash-Dibbeen, on the artery road leading to Ajloun | tel. 02 6 35 13 01 | www.lebanese-house.com*

▶ Edible souvenirs: along the busy route leading north from Jerash **(112 C3) (∅ D4)** farmers sell dried fruit and vegetables of usually excellent quality at good prices *(3–6 JD per kilo)*. Dried tomatoes and figs make lovely small presents for friends and relatives at home.

JERASH

TRIUMPHAL ARCH

The first monument you get to from the car park is the Triumphal Arch, built in AD 129 for Emperor Hadrian. The monument was situated outside the city wall, 3.5km/2mi long. From here, follow the Hippodrome in the direction of the southern gate.

SOUTHERN GATE

The Southern Gate has the visitor centre and a restaurant, as well as being the official entrance. Dating from the 2nd century, the lower part of the gate columns feature finely carved stone foliage. Immediately left when you come in you'll see an olive press dating back to the 3rd century.

OVAL FORUM

Situated behind the Southern Gate, the unusual form of the Oval Forum has puzzled archaeologists for a long time. Presumably the idea had been to connect the Temple of Zeus with the northern Roman theatre at the other end of town by a north-south axis. The hill on which the Temple of Zeus was built had been used for centuries previously to worship the gods. The forum was probably laid out for religious and ceremonial rituals.

MUSEUM

You'll see many interesting finds exhibited here, including jewellery, coins and theatre tickets made from fired clay. *April–Oct daily 8.30am–7pm, Nov–March daily 8.30am–4pm, public holidays 10am–3pm | free admission*

TEMPLE OF ZEUS 🔆

A large set of steps used to lead to the Temple of Zeus up on a hill to the left. Built in the 2nd century on the ruins of a Greek temple, it has suffered fairly extensive damage since.

SOUTHERN THEATRE

The well-restored theatre with 32 rows of seats was able to accommodate about 5000 spectators. In the first rows you can still see the engraved names of some donors. The best way to appreciate the theatre is by climbing the steps, which gives you a

Splendidly ornate architecture: Gerasa's Southern Theatre

✺ INSIDER TIP wide-ranging view of the ancient city and Jerash. The stage and entrances bear ornaments in the Corinthian style.

CARDO MAXIMUS

Leading away from the Oval Forum, the city's main artery is an 800m/900yd avenue, lined by 200 columns, most of them Corinthian. The reason that the original cobblestones are uneven is that the drainage system runs below it. The places where a stone is missing gives you a glimpse of the drain. The ruts left behind by the wooden wheels of the Roman chariots can be clearly made out still. Along this once resplendent boulevard you'll find the city's most important monuments. Before the first crossroads lies a round *agora,* or market place. Beyond that lie the sacred buildings.

CATHEDRAL

In the 4th century, a cathedral was erected on the site of a temple dedicated to Dionysus; this was the headquarters of the Bishop of Gerasa. Note the shrine with the Virgin Mary and the archangels Gabriel and Michael at the foot of the flight of steps.

NYMPHAEUM

All that is left of this two-storey 2nd-century well sanctuary is the monumental façade. The lower part was decorated with green marble, the upper with painted stucco.

TEMPLE OF ARTEMIS

This well-preserved and imposing temple dedicated to the patron saint of the city formed part of a large complex comprising steps, terraces and courtyards. Steps lead into the innermost sanctuary, which was only accessible to the priests. Its large dimensions (23 x 40m/75 x 130ft) made the temple one of the city's most important monuments.

THREE CHURCHES

Behind the temple you'll discover three of the over 153 churches that were erected following Christianisation. Built between AD 529 and 533, they are dedicated to John the Baptist, George, and Cosmas and Damian. Look out for the restored floor mosaics in the *Church of Cosmas and Damian* and the *Church of St John the Baptist*.

NORTHERN THEATRE

Noticeably smaller than the one at the southern entrance, this theatre, which hasn't been restored, only used to hold about 1600 spectators. An alternative way to walk back to the southern entrance is the INSIDER TIP dirt track on a rise leading west from the Northern Theatre through the meadows behind the Temple of Artemis.

FOOD & DRINK

RESTHOUSE

With its location right on the southern gate and a large dining room, the restaurant is geared towards groups of tourists.

WHERE TO STAY

OLIVE BRANCH RESORT ✺

Attractive location, pool, otherwise basic furnishings. Approx. 8km/5mi outside Jerash on the road to Ajloun, to the right of the main road, signposted. *30 rooms | tel. 02 6 34 05 55 | www.olivebranch.com. jo | Moderate*

WHERE TO GO

Situated between Jerash and Ajloun, the ● *Dibbin Nature Reserve* (112 C4) (*ⓜ D4*) makes for a good spot to take a break and enjoy an idyllic picnic under shade-giving pines and oaks. The park is very popular with the Ammanites.

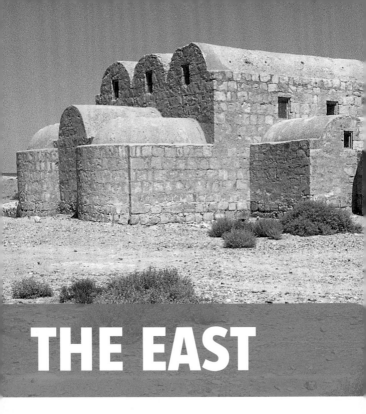

THE EAST

Leaving Amman in an easterly direction takes travellers to a part of the country which at first glance doesn't seem too inviting, with trucks dominating the desert highways leading to Iraq and Saudi Arabia.

The land connection via Jordan is in fact one of Iraq's vital arteries. However, the immense desert landscape – sometimes dried-out wetlands with a thick crust of salt, sometimes black basalt scree – has more to offer: along the two roads crossing the area like a ribbon you'll discover the famous Umayyad castles. It is their lack of pomp in particular that makes these modest buildings dating back to the 8th century small gems that are well worth a day trip. Here, wall paintings from the early Islamic period have survived, featuring, wait for it, naked women.

Originally from Damascus, the Umayyad rulers would hold court in these castles, settling legal disputes and fostering connections with the local Bedouin tribes that represented their power base. Yet these dwellings probably also served as places of pleasure, the remote desert providing the stage for banquets with wine, women and song, as they say.

Examples of pre-Islamic poetry, where sensual pleasures and alcohol play a major role, have come down to us too. The numerous representations of animals are proof that hunting gazelles and ducks, as well as physical exercise, were part of their lifestyle. When the

Photo: Qasr Amra desert castle

Time travel into the desert –
grazing water buffalo alongside
enchanting Umayyad castles

Abbasids defeated the Umayyads in AD 750, they transferred the capital to Bagdad. The region that today is Jordan declined in importance, and the desert castles were forgotten.

The tour to the castles is best undertaken by rental car or taxi, as they are extremely difficult to reach by public transport. If you have more time, stay the night in the small town of Azraq, which is surrounded by several nature reserves.

AZRAQ

(113 F5) *(ﬞ F5)* **This sleepy little town (pop. 4000) 110km/68mi east of Amman lives off the trade passing through. Heading north would take you to Iraq, south in the direction of Saudi Arabia.**

Back in the era of the caravans, the oasis of Azraq was a strategic hub for trade between the Saudi Arabian peninsula and Mesopotamia, as well as with Syria.

Early Islamic wall paintings in
the Umayyad castle of Qasr Amra

porting water buffaloes, crocodiles and foxes. However, since the 1980s, water has been pumped out of the only water reservoir in Jordan's eastern desert in order to supply Amman with drinking water, which has led to ecological collapse. The former swamp has now been reconstituted on an area spanning 12 sq km/4.5 sq mi; visitors can hike through it on a wooden boardwalk. Millions of migratory birds rest their weary wings here in winter, and if you're lucky, you might even catch a water buffalo in the high and dense reeds. A small exhibition illustrates the variety of fauna which used to roam here. Approx. 12km/7mi south of Azraq in the direction of Saudi Arabia, you'll find the ☺ INSIDER TIP Shawmari Desert Reserve, Jordan's first nature park (1975). Ostriches, the oryx antelope with its long horns and other wild animals have been resettled here. *Azraq Wetland Reserve visitor centre | tel. 05 3 83 52 25 | daily 9am–6pm | admission nature reserve 7 JD | bike hire 11 JD per day | www.rscn.org.jo/wildjordan | tel. 05 3 83 52 25 | www.rscn.org.jo*

FOOD & DRINK

Along the road leading towards Qasr al-Azraq, the *Azraq Tourist Palace Restaurant (daily | Budget)* is prepared for groups of tourists. At the *Azraq Resthouse (daily | Budget)* along the same road, you can eat on a shady terrace.

SIGHTSEEING

NATURE RESERVES
Right next to the town, the Royal Society for the Conservation of Nature (RSCN) has established the ★ ☺ *Azraq Wetlands Reserve*. Surprised? The bone-dry landscape that today spreads out in front of visitors used to be a swamp sup-

WHERE TO STAY

AZRAQ LODGES ☺
What was once a British field hospital is unrecognisable as such now: the architect Ammar Khammash has integrated the former main building into a futuristic-looking hotel built from concrete. Cloth sun-sails give the place a

link to Bedouin culture. The hotel is run by the RSCN. At the visitor centre you may book INSIDER TIP safari tours with the environmentalists: on foot, by bike or bus (3 people minimum). *16 rooms | signposted along the main road | contact for the Azraq Lodge and the neighbouring Shawmari Camp: room reservations tel. 05 3 83 50 17 | www.rscn.org.jo/wild jordan | Moderate*

WHERE TO GO

Opening times of the desert castles: *April–Oct daily 8am–5pm / 6pm, Nov–March daily 8am–4pm*

QASR AMRA ★ (113 E6) (*Ø E5*)

This complex (also called Qusair Amra) is the best-preserved of the desert castles and has been listed as a Unesco World Heritage site since 1999. Caliph Walid I had this hunting pavilion with bath house built in the 8th century; it would also have served as a pleasure palace. From the outside, the modest building displays enchantingly harmonious round forms, with the yellowish rock fitting well into the sandy landscape. The well in front of the entrance, 24m/80ft deep, supplied water to the *hammam*. Inside, the ● unique frescoes tell of the Damascene way of life at the time. The life-like paintings depict human figures – which in later Islamic art would become a rarity – and, even more unusually, naked women. No wonder that the Abbasids who followed the Umayyads in power denounced the 'debauchery' of their predecessors. Thanks to the remoteness of this little castle, subsequent iconoclasts overlooked these testimonies of early Islam. Later Islamic art would work almost exclusively with geometric and floral motifs, as well as letters (calligraphy), as according to the majority of religious interpretations, the representation of human beings is prohibited in Islam.

In the three-aisled reception hall with its vaulted ceiling you can see a depiction of a naked woman bathing. Next to her you'll see representations of six rulers who were defeated by the Umayyads. Amongst the four named rulers are the Persian Chosroes (aka Khosrau), the Ethiopian king Negus and the Visigoth Roderic, who suffered defeat in 711. Don't forget to admire the wonderful ceiling frescoes, immortalising artisans such as carpenters, blacksmiths and masons.

From the hall, a narrow corridor leads into the bathroom, which is divided into three areas: the walls of the changing rooms are decorated with naïve drawings of gazelles, a bear playing the lute and other animals. The *tepidarium* (cooling-down room) shows a group of three women bathing as well as a hunting scene. The dome of the *caldarium* (thermal bath) features representations of the sky and signs of the zodiac.

QASR AL-AZRAQ ★ (113 F5) (*𝄞 F5*)

This castle became famous through one of its guests, who spent the winter of 1917–18 within the walls of the building: Lawrence of Arabia camped out here while preparing to storm Damascus. Built from black basalt, the castle is still an imposing presence, even if most of the upper storeys were destroyed by an earthquake in 1927. The oldest inscription is a dedication to the rulers Diocletian and Maximian, who between AD 285 and 305 jointly ruled the Roman Empire. The fort was renovated by the Ayyubids, probably in the 13th century. The mosque in the courtyard dates back to that era too.

QASR AL-HALLABAT (113 D4) (*𝄞 E4*)

Built by the Romans in the 2nd century, the fort was later used as a monastery by Byzantine monks. In the first half of the 8th century the Umayyads destroyed the edifice and built it anew, partly using basalt stones from the Byzantine-Roman settlement of *Umm al-Jimal* (some 30km/18mi north). Today, there is only a moderately well-preserved ruin. Of the *Hammam as-Sarakh*, the bath serving Qasr al-Hallabat only a few miles away, only a few walls of the bathhouse and changing rooms are left. The water pipes can be made out easily.

QASR AL-KHARANA
(113 E6) (*𝄞 E6*)

Fortress or caravanserai? To this day it's not clear what purpose this well-preserved and clearly structured desert castle fulfilled. The large kitchen spaces as well as the stables for camels or horses around the courtyard suggest that it was some kind of desert hotel. The first floor is a maze of rooms and chambers. The terrace affords ☼ INSIDER TIP ▶ far-reaching views across the desert. The sturdy corner towers might suggest a defensive structure, yet the small openings in the exterior walls served as ventilation rather than as embrasures to fire through. The Kufic inscription above a door in the upper floor points to AD 711 as the year of construction.

QASR AL-MUSHATTA
(112 C6) (*𝄞 D5*)

Those who have visited the Pergamon Museum in Berlin will recognise the most beautiful part of this castle: the stuccoed southern façade has been on view there since 1903, when the Ottoman Sultan Abdel Hamid II gifted it to Emperor Wilhelm of Germany. There are plans to affix a replica to the original as part of a German-Jordanian co-operation. What remains of this desert castle, once the largest of its kind, are the mighty external walls, each 144m long and endowed with semi-circular towers. The palace is situated in a less than idyllic location in an area occupied by the international airport of Amman.

LOW BUDGET

▶ The simple restaurants for truck drivers from Iraq and Saudi Arabia cluster in the southern part of the small town of Azraq (113 F5) (*𝄞 F5*). Everybody sits together at big tables and orders the one dish that's available. Rule of thumb: the busier the place, the better the quality.

▶ Low-cost sightseeing: admittance to the desert castles is free – all the tourist guide expects is a 1 JD tip.

Life in the desert: a shepherd with his herd at Qasr al-Kharana

UMM AL-JIMAL ● (113 D3) (⌀ E4)

Umm al-Jimal ('Mother of the Camels') is one of Jordan's most important archaeological sites. Not far from the crossroads of several ancient trade routes, Nabataeans settled as far back as the 1st century AD. Later, the Romans expanded the place into a border town of military significance. One of the reasons Umm al-Jimal is so important in archaeological terms is the fact that it holds some of the oldest Christian churches. Part of the fascination of this place is that day-to-day life occupies centre stage here. How did the people live in the Roman, Byzantine and early Islamic periods? How did they organise the food supply? How did they manage to lay out complex water-supply systems and even to build small skyscrapers? What caused up to 5000 people to live in this apparently inhospitable place? And why was Umm al-Jimal abandoned for nearly 1000 years from around 750 AD onwards?

Starting in the 1970s, most of the remains of the town have been excavated and documented under the leadership of archaeologist Bert de Vries. The excellently presented website (see below) offers a virtual guided walk and extensive information on the plans that lie in store for Umm al-Jimal. One of the ideas is for a museum. To avoid the hottest part of the day, try to arrive before 11am or after 3pm. *Sun–Thu 8am–5pm | free admission | www.ummeljimal.org*

THE WEST

Are you asking yourself where the vegetables come from in this desert country? Your eyes are keen to feast on some juicy greenery once more? Take a trip into the Jordan Valley, the fruit and vegetable garden of the country.

Along the Jordan River, which forms the border with Israel and the Palestinian territories, plantations and gardens extend alongside green fields and juicy pastures. Here you can watch farmers at work. Rather then retrained Bedouins they are mostly Egyptians who have turned their back on the Nile Valley for the higher wages offered in Jordan.

However, in this country of contrasts the life-giving wealth of nature comes to a sudden end. In the south of the valley, the Jordan River meets the Dead Sea, where no living organism can survive. The mountains rising up steeply straight from its banks are barren and inhospitable. Due to the high salt and mineral content of the 'sea', a swim at the lowest point on earth provides a unique experience: even non-swimmers cannot drown. Still, if you're travelling with small children, stick to the pool, as an inadvertent 'sip' from the Dead Sea can be dangerous, particularly if the salt water gets into the respiratory tract.

Another attraction in the Jordan Valley is the site where Jesus Christ wa baptised: according to the most recent research it was probably on the eastern banks of the Jordan River rather than on the Palestinian side.

Photo: Olive trees in the Jordan Valley

Green orchards and barren mountain slopes – discover the site where Jesus was baptised, between the fertile Jordan Valley and the salty Dead Sea

JORDAN VALLEY

(112 B2–6) (⌂ C3–5) **The fertile valley owes its name to the Jordan River, which has its source in the Lebanese mountains.**

If you expect a raging torrent, you'll be disappointed: thanks to the heavy water use in the upper river valley in Israel, the Jordan on this stretch has shrunk to a narrow rivulet. Arguments about water keep flaring up between Jordan and Israel. The lush vegetation is only in part due to the Jordan River: in truth, it is the King Abdullah Canal which allows regular irrigation. The canal is fed by the Yarmouk river and from reservoir dams. The hot and humid climate allows three harvests per year, and the valley provides three quarters of Jordan's agricultural production. Wheat, barley, tomatoes, cucumbers and many types of fruit are cultivated here. However, highly subsidised

Al-Maghtas: much evidence suggests that this is indeed the very place where Jesus was baptised

water prices for the plantation owners lead to projects that make no ecological sense whatsoever: although bananas require extremely high amounts of water, for instance, the valley is covered in banana plantations. Increasing salinification, especially of the southern part of the Jordan Valley, forces ever-new experiments, with ever fewer plants actually able to thrive here.

SIGHTSEEING

PELLA ★ ● ☷ (112 B3) (*Ø C3*)

Next to the village of *Tabaqat Fahl*, the ruins of Pella are what remains of one of the cities of the Greek Decapolis. In around 310 BC, veterans of Alexander the Great's army settled on this hill, which had been inhabited for millennia already. The city had its heyday under Byzantine rule, when around 20,000 people lived here, including a bishop in residence. While excavations began as early as 1967, there is not a lot to

see in Pella compared with Umm Qais or Jerash: remains of the city wall and a basilica with 6th-century columns, as well as those of a theatre seating 400, have so far been exposed. The views of the Jordan Valley are stupendous. In spring, poppies and the black iris are in bloom – the best time for interesting hiking tours (take the hiking guide by Di Taylor and Tony Howard). For sustenance, the ☷ *Pella Resthouse (daily | tel. 02 6 56 08 99 | Moderate)* serves fine Arab cuisine with spectacular views from the terrace. Owner Deeb Gawahreh also manages a simple hotel in Pella (*11 rooms | Dheebgawahreh575@hotmail. com | Budget)*. Another accommodation option can be found between Umm Qais and Pella, 3km/2mi north of Sheikh Hussein. This is where the environmental organisation Friends of the Environment Middle East (FOEME) has set up a campsite with air-conditioned cottages (with Wi-Fi). Don't forget to reserve in good time (*10 rooms sleeping 28 guests | tel.

06 5 86 66 02 | jordanecopark.wordpress. com | *Budget–Moderate*).

BAPTISM SITE OF JESUS
(AL-MAGHTAS) ★ (112 B5) (*ﬡ C5*)

Excavations on this hill had to wait for the signing of the peace agreement with Israel in 1994. Before that, this was a military exclusion area covered in land-mines. Since 1997, Jordanian archaeologists have revealed several Early Christian churches, a monastery and baptismal fonts from the first centuries AD in the area. More recent research assumes that John the Baptist and the prophet Elijah were active here. This is supposed to be the site of 'Bethany-beyond-the-Jordan', where John was baptising' (Gospel of St John 1:28). The astounding correspondences between the scripture, reports by Christian pilgrims and archaeological finds are in favour of the hypothesis that the site where Jesus was baptised is probably indeed here. On *Elija's Hill (Tel al-Kharrar)* you can see the remains of a monastery as well as a complex system of cisterns and basins that probably served for mass baptisms. The surrounding area has hundreds of caves that used to be inhabited by hermits or monks.

Through the wild vegetation of *Wadi al-Kharrar,* where five springs have their source, a 2km/1.25mi INSIDER TIP foot-path leads down to the banks of the Jordan. Visitors may also visit the individual sights scattered across the extensive area aboard a minibus. One site is the remains of a 6th-century church where the Jordan runs in broad loops and has altered its course over the centuries. Two more churches, a bit further up, were established within the following 100 years. Finally you reach the main arm of the River Jordan. Only a few metres separate it from the Palestinian territories, occupied by Israel, on the other bank of the river.

The arguments supporting the thesis that the 'cradle of Christianity' lay on the eastern banks of the Jordan are recapitulated on the website *www.baptismsite.com*. In spring 2008, King Abdullah II donated land to build a new church. The visitor centre has a modern, air-conditioned *restaurant (Moderate)* with Arab cuisine. *April–Oct daily 8am–6pm, Nov–March daily 8am–4pm, last admittance 1 hr before closing time | admission 12 JD (incl. guide and minibus) | visitor centre tel. 05 3 59 03 60*

WHERE TO STAY

INSIDER TIP ▶ MOUNTAIN BREEZE COUNTRY CLUB ↯ (112 B5) (*ﬡ C5*)
Scenic campsite with restaurant (summer terrace with panoramic views, in winter curl up in style next to the fireplace). Children's play area, many sports options for children and adults, including archery and ball games. Careful:

★ Pella
The remains of the ancient city in their enchanting location
→ p. 58

★ Baptism site of Jesus (Al-Maghtas)
Early Christian baptismal font and hermits' caves – this is where John the Baptist and the prophet Elijah are said to have been active → p. 59

★ Dead Sea
Reading a newspaper in the salt-saturated sea without drowning in the process – that's part of any holiday in Jordan
→ p. 60

MARCO POLO HIGHLIGHTS

there's a paintball club too! All this action on offer coupled with outstanding gastronomic treats make this a good choice for a day trip too. Reservations required. Tents sleep up to five people (bring a sleeping bag). Chalets sleeping 2–4 guests are being planned. Breakfast is included in the price. For a description of how to get there, see the club's homepage. *Daily 10am–10pm, April–Oct often longer | tel. 077 723 45 69 | www.jordan adventure.com | Moderate*

DEAD SEA

(112 A–B6, 118 B1–2) (*C5–7*) ★ Coming directly from Amman, the 45km/28mi-long a road down to the Dead Sea covers a difference in altitude **of 1300m/4265ft with many hairpin bends.**

At the end of the road you're at the lowest point on earth, the Dead Sea, 400m/1310ft below sea level. The inland sea is 75km/46mi long and 16km/10mi wide. While certainly 'dead', in that it contains no life except a few microbes, its ecology is threatened. Every year, the level of the Dead Sea sinks by one metre, as the inflow from the Jordan River and mountain springs is diverted for drinking water or agriculture. Furthermore, the Israeli and Jordanian industrial facilities (potash and beauty aids from natural products) at the southern end use up large amounts of water.

Environmental activists fear that by 2050 this inland sea might shrink to half of its present size if nothing is done. For years

BOOKS & FILMS

▶ **Story of a City. A Childhood in Amman** – the economist and novelist Abdelrachman Munif describes the Jordanian capital as it was in the 1940s

▶ **Our Last Best Chance** – The Pursuit of Peace in a Time of Peril – King Abdullah II tells the story of his life (2011). Naturally, some of the historical interpretations are coloured by subjectivity; this is not the only perspective on matters. Yet the book affords glimpses of the personality and way of thinking of the Jordanian king

▶ **Lawrence of Arabia** – Cinematic classic by David Lean starring Peter O'Toole in 1962, partly filmed at original locations in Wadi Rum. The story is about the famous British orientalist and adventurer T E Lawrence and the situation in Arabia shortly before the foundation of the Jordanian state

▶ **Captain Abu Ra'ed** – The first Jordanian feature film, made in 2007 by Amin Matalqa. The protagonist is a widower working as part of a team of cleaners at the airport. One day the children from his neighbourhood prise him out of his routines and he befriends a young female pilot. A moving story told in beautiful images

▶ **Recycle** – In this 2006 film, Dutch-Jordanian director Mahmoud Al Massad tells the story of a former Al Qaida sympathiser who returns to Jordan to try and rebuild his life

there has been talk about building a canal to channel water from the Red Sea into the Dead Sea. However, the tense political situation in the region hinders cooperation projects between Jordan, Israel and Palestinians.

At about 30 per cent, the salt content of the Dead Sea is nearly ten times as high as that of other seas. The water often has miraculous effects on skin conditions and rheumatism and is attracting ever more health tourists. Don't miss out on a INSIDER TIP full-body mud pack. The grey mud can be found in depressions in the water near the shore or is made available at the hotels. Apply the mud and let it dry – after rinsing it off later, your skin will be silky soft.

FOOD & DRINK – WHERE TO STAY

DEAD SEA SPA HOTEL
This hotel, the oldest on the Dead Sea, housed the negotiations for the peace agreement between Jordan and Israel. Renovated since, the hotel is popular with children, boasting several pools with a climbing frame and a large water slide. More basic and cheaper than the other luxury hotels. Non-residents may use the pools and beach, paying 30 JD per person (children 15 JD). *272 rooms | tel. 05 3 56 10 00 | www.dssh.jo | Expensive*

KEMPINSKI HOTEL ISHTAR DEAD SEA ☀
A more recent addition to the luxury hotels on the Dead Sea. Gardens and lagoons, small rivers and waterfalls – and all that right in the middle of the desert! Attractive sports facilities and numerous spa treatments are on offer. The babysitting and childminding services are a plus. Nice for guests' privacy, less so for those not lucky enough to be holidaying here:

A body wrap with mud from the Dead Sea is bliss for the skin

non-residents have no access to the hotel beach. *117 rooms and suites | Swaimeh, Dead Sea Road | tel. 05 3 56 88 88 | www.kempinski.com/de/deadsea | Expensive*

MÖVENPICK
This gorgeous luxury complex aims at look of a traditional Bedouin village. Stretching from the main building to the sea, the bungalows are swathed in bougainvillea and oleander. The ground-floor rooms have their own terrace. Insist on being housed in that part and not in the main building. From the ☀ swimming pool you have a fantastic view across

Dead Sea Beach: conservative Jordanians keep things under wraps even while swimming

the Dead Sea. Narrow, rocky beach. For a supplement, the spa offers massages, mud baths and other beauty treatments. Those who only want to use the pool and beach for the day pay 40 JD per person to get in, 50 JD at weekends (incl. 20 JD for food and drink). *346 rooms | Sweimeh, Dead Sea | tel. 05 3 56 11 11 | www.moeven pick-deadsea.com | Expensive*

MUJIB CHALETS

Not cheap, yet a lot cheaper than the five-star hotels and blessed with a fantastic view: the RSCN's Mujib Chalets at the exit from Wadi Mujib, a 30-minute drive south of Sweimeh. The double rooms with their own terrace and shared showers cost around 50 JD per person, single rooms approx. 70 JD. Non-residents may use the beach paying 10 JD. *Tel. 06 46 16 52 30 | www.rscn.org.jo | Moderate*

BEACHES

Swimming is allowed nearly everywhere on the rocky shore. However, as it is im-

perative that you wash off the salt water afterwards, look out for a beach with showers.

WHERE TO GO

WADI FEYNAN (114 B5) (*m* C9)

The INSIDER TIP road leading south along the Dead Sea is much prettier than the desert highway. In *Wadi Araba* you can see Jordan's only fine sand dunes. On this route you may want to overnight at the ● 😊 INSIDER TIP Feynan Eco Lodge, formerly an RSCN project and one of the world's best eco-hotels, with views of the desert landscape from the terrace. From the Dead Sea you drive to the meeting point at the village of Qurayqira (pronounced Gry-gra – for a precise itinerary from all directions see *www.feynan.com*). Should your car have no 4WD, you'll have to leave the vehicle in Qurayqira and organise a pick-up for a supplement of around 15 JD (let staff know when booking!). The drive takes around

30 minutes. The remote hotel runs on solar energy and is lit with romantic candles in the evening. The rooms have no power points. Internet connections are not stable; bring cash for paying your stay, as the card readers often fail due to lack of electricity and radio connections. Food is purely vegetarian, and the entire hotel is non-smoking.

The hotel is a good base for scenic walks through the rock landscape, to Dana and even to Petra (see chapter 'The Kings Highway'). There are no direct road connections to Dana, but you can have yourself picked up there. *(Eco Lodge | 26 en-suite rooms in three categories | closed July and Aug | lodge tel. 079 7 48 79 00, reservations in Amman tel. 06 4 64 55 80 | www.feynan.com | Moderate).*

This area, which was settled as far back as 10,000 years ago, boasts several archaeological sites. This was the site of the largest copper mines in the Levant, which were worked for over 5000 years (from 4000 BC to around AD 1500). Reminders of this are large heaps of detritus. On view are also the remains of hydraulic equipment, left over from the copper smelting works of the Romans and Byzantines.

WADI MUJIB (114 B–C2) (*ℳ C6–7*)

Several hiking trails lead through Wadi Mujib *(usable between April and Oct)*, amongst them the *Siq Trail*, the *Ibex Trail* and the *Malaqi Trail*. Nearly all hiking trails start at the Dead Sea and end there too. A trekking tour into the narrow wadi where you swim parts of the trail through warm water is an extraordinary natural experience. Truly courageous trekking fans and experienced climbers may choose to INSIDER TIP cross the canyon from above – only with a guide, however. Professionally guided tours are offered by several outfits, amongst them Wild Jordan (RSCN, *www.rsch.org.jo*) and Terhaal *(www.terhaal.com)*. If you are travelling with your own car, the hikes crossing the Mujib Canyon from above start in Fagua, a village between Madaba and Karak (meeting point: RSCN office). Starting from Fagua, the trek is approx. 15km/9mi long, taking 6–8 hours, depending on your level of fitness. If required, transport back to Fagua may be organised for you.

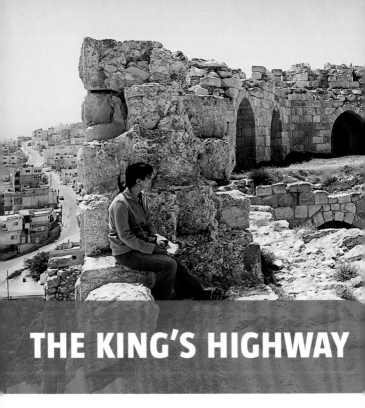

THE KING'S HIGHWAY

The King's Highway (Tariq al-Sultani) is one of the most beautiful routes leading from Amman to Aqaba. Snaking along the border between the Wadi Araba section of the Jordan Rift Valley and the high plateau of the desert, it offers stunning landscapes.

From Mount Nebo, the King's Highway leads via Madaba, the spectacular Wadi Mujib (aka 'Jordan's Grand Canyon', with the legendary Trajan Resthouse at its southern end), the Dana Nature Reserve and the Crusader castles of Karak and Shobak to the famous Nabataean city of Petra. The King's Highway supposedly corresponds to the route that Moses is said to have taken to lead the Israelites to the Promised Land. Later, the caravans of the Nabataeans travelled this way laden with incense and precious stones.

After Emperor Trajan had integrated the Nabatean Empire into the Roman Empire in AD 106, he set to work on extending the Via Nova Traiana, leading from Damascus to Aqaba: the King's Highway was transformed from a caravan trail into a paved road with milestones and all. Take a trip through the millennia where – unless you visit Petra – you will meet few tourists.

DANA

(114 B5) (*ⁿ* C9) ★ ☀ ☺ Do try and include a stay in the Dana Nature Reserve in your travel plans. The canyon

Simply spectacular – from Mount Nebo through the canyon landscape of Dana to Crusader castles and the rock city of Petra

landscape with its round rocks in many tones of colours holds one of Jordan's most beautiful natural spectacles.

Several hiking routes are marked by stones, yet it is worth your while taking a guide. Established in 1989, the nature reserve covering 320 sq km /120 sq mi is the largest in the country. 600 species of plants, 190 species of birds and 37 further animal species can be found here *(admission nature reserve 7 JD)*. Established in the 15th century, the *Dana Village*, built entirely of stone and clay,

lies on a rocky outcrop above Wadi Dana. The view from above during the drive there is nothing short of breathtaking. The village was almost completely abandoned for a while, as the families moved to Qadisiya on the main road. This explains the fact that some of the houses and stables are now fallen down. However, thanks to a project run by environmentalists, a few families have either stayed in Dana or have resettled here. This is a fascinating place to while away a few hours.

The drive to Karak through Wadi Mujib opens up stunning vistas

FOOD & DRINK – WHERE TO STAY

DANA GUESTHOUSE ☼ ☺

The nature conservancy organisation's hotel scores with its spectacular views, which do however come at a price. The tasteful common room and the terrace lie right above the wadi. Good food, in winter cosy evenings at the fireplace with board games. Even if you're housed in a different hotel, try and visit for dinner one day *(book in advance, opens by arrangement!)*, to enjoy the beautiful views. *9 rooms | tel. 03 2270498 | dhana@rscn.org.jo | Moderate*

INSIDER TIP DANA HOTEL ☺

This down-to-earth place without a pool is located right in the town, opposite the attractive little mosque where the call to prayer does not yet come canned. The hotel is run by the village residents, meaning the people benefit directly. The simply furnished, basic rooms with pretty metal beds are grouped around a courtyard. Bedouin tent on the ☼ roof terrace. *7 rooms | tel. 03 2270537 | Budget*

RUMMANA CAMP ☼ ☺

Access to the nature reserve can also be had through the Rummana campsite (turn right shortly before the village of Qadisiya), a project managed by the local population. Here you can stay the night in 20 shared tents equipped with mattresses, amidst an unspoiled landscape. The hiking trails begin right outside your tent door, and admission to the nature reserve is included in the accommodation price. Barbecue areas are available, but you can also choose the catering option. *Tel. 03 2270498 | dhana@rscn.org.jo | closed Nov–15 March | Moderate*

INFORMATION

The visitor centre with sales room is situated next to the Dana Guesthouse. You may book guides here for hiking tours or take the shuttle bus to the Rummana campsite. *Daily 8am–3pm | tel. 03 2 27 04 98 | www.rscn.org.jo*

KARAK

(114 C3) (ⓜ C7) **The drive to Karak leads through an exciting landscape. In long hairpin bends, the a road winds its way through Wadi Mujib 1000m/3300ft further below, which at this point is very wide.**

The town of Karak is dominated by the Crusader castle higher up.

SIGHTSEEING

KARAK FORT ★
The imposing, completely renovated fort is an impressive example of the military architecture of the Crusaders. Baldwin I, who after the death of his brother Godfrey of Bouillon became king of the Crusader state of Jerusalem, built the castle in 1142. The determining factor in

his choice of location was possibly that the majority of the inhabitants of Karak were Christian Arabs. In 1189, following a siege lasting one year the Crusaders had to surrender to the Arab commander Salah ed-Din, who had starved the fort into submission. As the Egyptian ruler Ibrahim Pasha had the castle walls destroyed, the upper storeys are only ruins now. However, the ☼ additions from Mamluk times yield wonderful views. The most interesting feature is the subterranean banquet halls, which remained undamaged. *Daily 8am–5pm | admission 1 JD*

FOOD & DRINK

KIR HERES
A recommended establishment right in front of the fort. Tasty Arab and international dishes. Owner Rashid Dmour himself looks after his guests. *Daily | Castle Street | tel. 03 2 35 55 95 | Moderate*

★ **Dana**
Exciting travel experience amidst a colourful rock landscape, varied flora and fauna, and romantic sandstone houses → p. 64

★ **Karak Fort**
In the subterranean halls of this imposing fort Crusaders once made merry → p. 67

★ **St George's Church**
The Palestine mosaic in Madaba shows the world as it was 1500 years ago, as well as enchanting depictions of plants and animals → p. 69

★ **Mount Nebo**
Overwhelming view of the Promised Land from one of Jordan's most sacred Christian pilgrimage destinations → p. 70

★ **Umm ar-Rasas**
Byzantine floor mosaics and a hermit's tower – completely devoid of mod cons like an entrance or stairs → p. 71

★ **Petra**
Spectacular highlight of any trip to Jordan: the Nabataean city carved into the rock forms a unique symbiosis of nature and architecture → p. 71

MARCO POLO HIGHLIGHTS

MADABA

WHERE TO STAY

While the Crusader castle of Karak is an absolute highlight of any trip, accommodation options don't live up to this. The the Crusaders to this castle, which was also erected by Baldwin I. While restored by the Mamluks in the 14th century, the edifice today is in a relatively bad state. Over the coming years, Shobak will be

View of Madaba, a popular starting point for round trips through Jordan

best thing to do is to plan your sightseeing in such a way that you can travel on after lunch.

restored with the help of Italian experts from the University of Florence.

TOWER HOTEL
Rooms with shared bathroom. *18 rooms | Castle Street | tel. 03 2 35 42 93 | Budget*

MADABA

WHERE TO GO

INSIDER TIP ▶ SHOBAK ☼
(114 B6) (*∅ C9*)

Fans of castles should schedule a stop in Shobak to take in the significant fort occupying a proud position. Montreal (or Mons Realis) was the name given by

(112 B–C6) (*∅ C6*) **A few miles beyond Amman airport you'll see the turn for Madaba (pop. 40,000). For the past few years, this provincial town has been booming – not least as there is an American university here. The town is mentioned under the name Mebda in the Old Testament.**

Inhabited by a Christian majority, Madaba is famous for its mosaics. This ancient craft, which reached its apogee in Byzantine times, is kept alive in the mosaic school.

SIGHTSEEING

CHURCH OF THE APOSTLES

The mosaic floors of this church, built in 578, are amongst the most beautiful in Madaba – look out for the personified representation of the sea, featuring a woman emerging from the waves, surrounded by marine creatures. Note the cat, ready to jump, alongside the bird or the wolf ogling a grape! *Daily 8am–5pm | admission 2 JD (including the Madaba Museum and the Archaeological Park)*

ARCHAEOLOGICAL PARK

Open-air museum with the ruins of several churches and town palaces. What has remained are wonderful floor mosaics, for instance the representations of *Amor and Aphrodite* and the Greek tragedy of Phaedra who fell in love with her stepson Hippolytus *(Hippolytus Hall)*. *April–Sept daily 8am–7pm, Oct–March daily 8am–5pm | admission 2 JD (including the Church of the Apostles and the Madaba Museum)*

MADABA MUSEUM

The museum shows ceramics, jewellery, weapons and mosaics. *Oct–April daily 8am–5pm, May–Sept daily 8am–7pm | admission 2 JD (including the Church of the Apostles and the Archaeological Park)*

ST GEORGE'S CHURCH ⭐

This Greek Orthodox church, built in 1884 on the ruins of a Byzantine predecessor, shelters the famous ● Madaba Map of Palestine. Put together around AD 560 from 2 million stones, this map is the first geographical representation of the region still in existence. The floor mosaic was only rediscovered in the 19th century. Originally measuring 16 x 6 m/52 x 20ft, the map is heavily damaged today; still, you can make out Lower Egypt and the Nile Delta, Jerusalem and Sidon, in what is today Lebanon. The centre of the map is occupied by Jerusalem, clearly showing the city walls and the Damascus Gate. The playful animal and plant representations provide additional charm. Note how at the estuary of the River Jordan the fish are swimming away from the salty waters of the Dead Sea. *Daily 8am–7pm | admission 1 JD | King Talal Street*

FOOD & DRINK

AYOLA CAFE

Enjoy a sandwich and a fresh fruit juice sitting right opposite St George's Church on carpets at low tables. *Daily | King Talal Street | tel. 05 3 25 18 43 | Budget*

LOW BUDGET

▶ A curious labyrinthine hotel spread across several floors is the *Dana Tower Hotel*. From the pretty ☘ terrace you can see the entire village of Dana (114 B5) (*𝄂 C9*). Book your room with half-board as Dana has no restaurants (apart from the RSCN's fairly expensive Dana Guesthouse). *7 rooms | tel. 03 2 27 02 26 | reservations tel. 079 5 68 88 53 (Nabil) | dana_tower2@hotmail.com*

▶ The small *Petra Pearl Restaurant* (116 C1) (*𝄂 B10*) prepares an excellent shawarma (mutton doner kebab). *Coming from Petra turn right off the Obelisk Circle*

MADABA

HARET JDOUNA

This wonderful eatery near St George's Church consists of several traditional houses grouped around a shady courtyard. Fine Jordanian food is served inside, in the courtyard and on a roof terrace. *Daily | King Talal Street | tel. 05 3 24 86 50 | Moderate*

INFORMATION

You may use the car park of the *visitor centre* to leave your car. From here most sights are within walking distance. *300 m from Baladiya Circle | April–Oct daily 8am–7pm, Nov–March daily 8am–5.30pm | tel. 05 3 25 35 63*

WHERE TO STAY

MARIAM HOTEL

Centrally located mid-range hotel with a well-kept terrace area and a swimming pool. Family rooms with up to four

WHERE TO GO

BERG NEBO ★ ● ⅍
(112 B6) (*∅ C5–6*)

10km/6mi west of Madaba you'll find one of the most important Christian

Bathing in the hot thermal springs of Hammamat Ma'in

beds. Good value. *57 rooms | Aisha Um Al Mumeneen Street | tel. 05 3 25 15 29 | www.mariamhotel.com | Moderate*

INSIDER TIP SALOME HOTEL

Very clean and quiet, pretty terrace, excellent value, ideal for families. *34 rooms | Aisha Umm Al Mu'meneen Street | tel. 05 3 24 86 06 | www.salome hotel.com | Moderate*

pilgrimage sites in Jordan, Mount Nebo. From here Moses is said to have seen the Promised Land following the Exodus. On a clear day, you have an overwhelming view across the Dead Sea to Jericho; you might even be able to make out Jerusalem on the plateau on the horizon. Sunset is a particularly beautiful time to be here. The 840m/2755ft mountain has been a place of pilgrimage since the beginnings of Christendom. The Franciscans who bought part of the mountain in 1933 discovered the remains of a three-aisled *basilica* with impressive 6th-century floor mosaics: animal and plant motifs are joined by a hunter and a lion as well as a shepherd and his herd. *Visitor centre May–Sept 8am–7pm, Oct–April 8am–4.30pm | admission 1 JD*

HAMMAMAT MA'IN ☆
(114 B1) (𝓂 C6)
A bendy road offering pretty views leads into *Wadi Zarqa Ma'in*. Since the Roman era, the INSIDER TIP thermal springs have been attracting visitors and rheumatic patients. Natural stone basins invite you to take a bath in hot water fed in from a 25m/82ft waterfall. Be careful: when the water, containing sulphur, soda and magnesium, comes out of the ground, its temperature is up to 60°C / 140 °F. *Springs daily. 6am–4pm | admission 15 JD*
The *Evason Ma'in Hot Spring and Six Senses Spa* luxury hotel appears a bit chunky, yet the location is overwhelming. Book any spa treatments as a package, as purchased individually they quickly add up. Free shuttle to the Dead Sea (*97 rooms | tel. 05 3 24 55 00 | www.sixsenses .com/Evason-Ma-In | Expensive*)

HEROD'S FORT ☆ (114 B1) (𝓂 C6)
On a hill an approx. 30-minute drive south of Madaba, at the town of Mukawir, discover the fort of Herod Antipas. The climb is made easier by natural stone steps, but you do need sturdy footwear. Due to the sun, the best time to visit in spring and summer is from 3pm onwards. There are toilets, very basic catering but top parking facilities. This is also a suitable starting point for a hike to the Dead Sea. *Daily April–Oct 8am–6pm, Nov–March 8am–5pm | admission 2 JD*

UMM AR-RASAS ★ (114 C1) (𝓂 D6)
The ancient town of Kastron Mefaa was already mentioned in the Bible, inhabited by Romans and finally decorated with mosaics by Byzantine Christians. Most of the town approx. 32km/20mi south of Madaba has been destroyed; visitors come mainly to see the floor mosaics in the *Church of St Stephen* outside the perimeter of the city walls: this largest floor mosaic in the country shows 28 cities in Egypt, Jordan and Palestine. Representations of human figures have been destroyed by iconoclasts. A curiosity is the rectangular tower, 15m/50ft high, but without an entrance or any set of steps. Presumably it was built for a hermit who would have lived on the pillar at the top. Since 2004, this has been a Unesco World Heritage site. There are no direct public transport options to Umm ar-Rasas. Take the bus from Madaba to Dhiban, and from there carry on by taxi; alternatively arrive directly by car/taxi from Madaba going in the direction of Dhiban and follow signs from there. *Visitor centre (usually only the WCs are open) at the Church of St Stephen | daily 8am–5pm | free admission*

PETRA

DETAILED MAP ON PAGE 122–123
(116 C1) (𝓂 B10) ★ **The rock city of Petra is the highlight of any trip to Jordan. It would be impressive even just for the luminescent sandstone in tones of violet, red, pink, yellow, cream and brown, and the deep canyons and wadis.**
The Nabataeans strove to bring their magnificent architecture into harmony with this nature, carving the façades of their temples, treasure chambers, houses and tombs into the pinkish-red rock.

PETRA

Some 800 monuments are preserved in Petra and surroundings. The entrance to the rock city lies in the village of *Wadi Mussa*. In 2007 Petra was named one of the seven 'New Wonders of the World'. While in scientific terms, the Swiss initiative is somewhat controversial, the Jordanians are very proud of the accolade.

SIGHTSEEING

The sights are presented here in the sequence of the regular circular tour (*visitor centre at the entrance to the rock city | unless otherwise specified: daily April–Oct 6am–6pm, Nov–March 6am–4pm | admission 50 JD for non-Jordanians, applicable to any travellers not coming in via Eilat. Travellers coming in from Eilat who haven't been to Taba (Egypt) before pay 90 JD | www.petrapark.com/visitor-center*).

SIQ

First you walk to the entrance of the narrow rock crevasse, the Siq, wending its way between steep rock walls, jutting up 100m/330ft. On the way there to the right you'll see three freestanding *rock cubes,* probably block tombs dating back to the 1st century AD. As their function wasn't known, the Bedouin called them 'djinn' blocks, i.e. ghost tombs. Opposite you'll find the *obelisk tomb* and below that a classic Nabataean building with three rooms *(Triclinium),* presumably a hall that served for worshipping the dead. The 1.2km/0.75mi trail through the Siq, probably a former river bed, shows remains of the ancient Nabataean street paving, and on the walls you'll see what's left of the aqueducts.

TREASURY (AL-KHAZNE)

The first glimpse of the treasury when the rock crevasse opens up is absolutely stunning. Emerging from the dark of the ever-narrowing canyon you'll first spot part and finally the entire façade, 43m/141ft high, of the building. INSIDER TIP In the early morning, when the sun lights up the façade, it reveals the rock in its many luminous colours. The edifice was constructed in the 1st century BC as a tomb for a Nabataean king. The ornate-

Built by the Nabataeans and extended by the Romans: the theatre in Petra

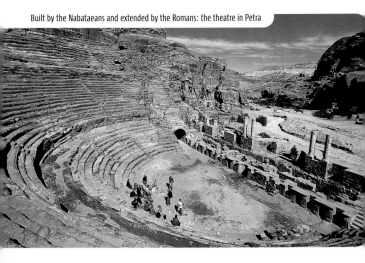

ly carved façade shows Nabataean gods. The building owes its name to the urn at the top, which the Bedouin assumed to hold valuable treasures.

THEATRE

At the treasury the gorge turns into the Street of Façades, lined with buildings, probably tombs, featuring fine stone-masonry work. Finally you reach the ☆ *theatre* carved in the rock. Built by the Nabataeans, it was expanded by the Romans to a 7000-seat capacity. The last rows of seats allow views of the valley basin.

ROYAL TOMBS

Opposite the theatre, a dozen tombs have been carved into the rock, partly one on top of the other. Their façades are amongst the most impressive of the roughly 500 tombs in Petra. Whether they were indeed created for kings is not known. The colossal *Urn Tomb* has a front courtyard and a large main chamber. This is where the Byzantines established a church in the 5th century, evidenced by an inscription inside. Next to it, the much smaller *Silk Tomb* owes its name to a wealth of colours: the rock appears grained in grey, white, blue and pink. The *Corinthian Tomb* has confused many archaeologists: the upper part is a reconstruction of the treasury, the lower a copy of the Triclinium at the Siq. The *Palace Tomb* next door is an imitation of a Roman palace with four gates and 18 columns – one of the largest and presumably most recent monuments of Petra.

STREET OF COLONNADES

Here you are right in the – relatively heavily damaged – heart of the town. The Romans paved this main street in the 2nd century and lined it with shops. Coming from the theatre you'll see to the right at the beginning of the Street of Colonnades the remains of the *Nymphaeum*. On the small rising to the right of the Cardo Maximus excavations are still underway to reveal a *Byzantine church* and the *Temple of Winged Lions*. The small detour to the 6th-century church is worthwhile for its `INSIDER TIP` fine floor mosaics. The columns of the temples were once indeed crowned by winged lions. The interior reveals the Nabataean fertility goddess Atargatis astride a dolphin.

QASR AL-BINT FARAUN

Anything the Bedouin couldn't figure out, they connected with the pharaohs. The Qasr al-Bint Faraun (Castle of the Pharaoh's Daughter), on the left at the end of the Street of Colonnades, is however a temple dedicated to the main Nabataean goddess Dushara. This most important sacred monument in Petra is the only one to have been erected as a freestanding building. It combines elements of oriental and Greek-Roman architecture.

MUSEUM

The museum next to the *Forum Resthouse* at the end of the Street of Colonnades shows a fine collection of steles, oil lamps, coins and jars. *April–Sept daily 8am–7pm, Oct–March 8am–4pm | free admission*

MOUNTAIN TOURS

More monuments are hidden in the surrounding mountains. While only accessible via partly steep paths, they are worth the effort. You might like to hire a donkey. *Monastery (Ed-Deir):* this tour is a must, even though it's one of the most demanding. Behind the *Forum Resthouse* at the end of the Street of Colonnades starts a set of 788 stairs. Once you reach Ed-Deir after a good hour or so, your last remaining breath will be taken away by an imposing, well-preserved monument, 40m/130ft high and 47m/154ft wide, hewn into the yellowish rock right in the heart of nature. The roof is crowned by a huge urn. The loneliness of the place

Obelisk on Petra's sacrificial site

makes for its particular charm, even if the monument is less finely worked than the treasury, Carry on walking for a few more metres to the ⚜ viewpoint to the left, to see Wadi Araba spread out at your feet. ⚜ Sacrificial site: approx. 200 m before you reach the theatre (coming from Siq), a small path branches off and leads in a half-hour climb to the sacrificial site. Atop the 1035m/3395ft summit are two obelisks (7m/23ft high) in honour of Nabataean deities. In order to create this site, the entire mountain top around them was chiselled away. The sacrificial site lies on a rocky ledge. The two altars were probably used for animal sacrifices. You can easily make out the drainage channels for the blood. From up here you enjoy the best view over Petra down in the valley basin. Descending south leads you past further sights: the *Lion Fountain* (water once flowed from the mouth of the lion and was channelled down into the city), the *Garden Tomb* and the *Tomb of the Roman Soldier* (named after the three statues above the entrance in Roman armour). You reach Petra at the Qasr al-Bint Faraun.

FOOD & DRINK

In ancient Petra itself only the *Forum Restaurant* offers an – expensive – lunch. Bring a picnic!

CLEOPATRA

Jordanian cuisine in a welcoming ambience. Try *maglouba*, a speciality involving mutton, rice and potatoes. *Wadi Mussa, main street* | Budget

INSIDER TIP ▶ PETRA KITCHEN ●

In this restaurant guests do part of the cooking themselves, under the guidance of chef Eid Nawafleh: workshops in Arab cuisine at accessible prices. Reservations required. *Tel. 03 215 46 66 | info@ jordantours-travel.com* | Moderate

ENTERTAINMENT

Petra at Night: an evening within the ruins of Petra, with candlelight, storytelling and Bedouin music – unforgettable! *Ticket 12 JD | three events a week, the visitor centre has the dates and times*
Seen enough? Why not partake of a drink at the INSIDER TIP Cave Bar in the Forum Hotel – in a cave dating back to Nabataean times. Particularly nice for a nightcap after a nocturnal hike. The ● Al Multaqa Lounge in the airy and light, richly decorated atrium of the exclusive

Mövenpick Resort is a fairy-tale place for a cocktail *(both Wadi Mussa, at the entrance gate to Petra)*.

WHERE TO STAY

INSIDER TIP **AMMARIN BEDOUIN CAMP**

Dive into the world of the Ammarin, 10km/6mi north of Petra. A small museum gives a glimpse of the way of life of these desert dwellers. The camp exudes a close-to-nature rustic vibe, and some of the Bedouin speak a little English. Longer camel trekking and shorter hiking tours are on offer, and there is a smaller archaeological site right next door to explore (Siq Albarid). *Tel. 079 9 75 55 51 | www.bedouincamp.net | Moderate*

HOTEL AMRA PALACE

Well-kept, clean mid-range hotel in Wadi Mussa. The ● Turkish bath is sheer bliss after a long dusty day of hiking (13 JD for guests, otherwise 20 JD), Indoor swimming pool. *72 rooms | tel. 03 215 70 70 | www.amrapalace.com | Moderate*

FORUM GUEST HOUSE HOTEL

Pretty, dependable mid-range hotel. Bright friendly rooms, good breakfast, welcoming ambience. Another plus is that you may use the pool of the Crowne Plaza Hotel next door. Book well in advance! *147 rooms | tel. 03 215 62 66 | www.crowneplaza.com | Moderate–Expensive*

SHARAH MOUNTAINS HOTEL

Clean, air-conditioned, central location on the main road; ask for rooms giving on to the back. *25 rooms | tel. 03 215 72 94 | sharahhostel@yahoo.com | Moderate*

TAYBET ZAMAN ☆

The complex is styled as a traditional village. Particularly beautiful: room 401 with its bed below a domed roof, and no. 406 with its views from the veranda. *105 rooms | Taybeh, approx. 9km/5mi south of Petra | tel. 03 215 01 11 | www.jordan tourismresorts.com | Expensive*

JEAN LOUIS BURCKHARDT

Visitors to the wonder of the world that is Petra may hardly believe that for centuries hardly anybody in Europe knew about the rock city and the highly advanced civilisation of the Nabataeans. Only a few explorers dared to travel the scarcely populated areas to the east of the Jordan River, dominated by Bedouin tribes. One of them was the universal scholar and naturalist Jean Louis Burckhardt. Born in 1784 in Lausanne, Switzerland, he first studied Arabic, law and mathematics, then started travelling the Middle East, Egypt and Sudan from 1809 onwards for the British African Association. The adventurous scholar gained the confidence of the locals by converting to Islam and calling himself 'Sheikh Ibrahim'. Burckhardt even took the pilgrimage to Mecca. Asked about his accent he would say that he was from India. In the summer of 1812, Burckhardt was one of the first Europeans to visit the city of Petra. His travel reports led the Europeans to recognise the immense historical and cultural importance of the region.

THE SOUTH

The far south of Jordan marks the end of monuments and weary sightseeing eyes. No more temples, churches or castles demand the visitor's attention.

As a reward for all that sightseeing, this region allows you to relax and give yourself over to nature: the unique desert landscape of Wadi Rum and the waves of the Red Sea with its spectacular underwater world in Aqaba – only one hour apart by car. Wadi Rum (pronounced as in the drink) enthuses fans of deserts even if they have seen many others: steep mountains reminiscent of cliffs jut up suddenly out of the reddish desert sand. If you've seen the film Lawrence of Arabia, you might at least have an idea what to expect, as parts of this cinematic masterpiece were filmed in Wadi Rum at the original locations.

If you have the feeling that the fine desert sand gets into every single pore, it might be time to head to Aqaba. The first swim in the crystal-clear waters of the Red Sea is unforgettable bliss even if your mind, by now pampered by natural beauty, might struggle at first to get used to the container port and industrial facilities. Still, snorkelling or diving in the coral reefs, with wealth of fish and colours beyond compare, will quickly reconcile you. With a bit of luck you might spot dolphins or even whales in the Gulf of Aqaba.

Photo: Divers in the Red Sea

Red desert sand and turquoise water –
from the star-studded sky above Wadi Rum
to the underwater world of the Red Sea

AQABA

(116 B5) (*∅ A13*) **Aqaba (pop.
100,000) is Jordan's only port and only
access to the sea. This strip of coast is
26km/16mi long – but only because
Saudi Arabia donated 12km/7.5mi in a
1965 land swap.**
On the other side of the bay lies the
Israeli resort of Eilat. The lack of space
explains why tourist beaches, container
terminal and the phosphate industry lie

> **WHERE TO START?**
> **Royal Yacht Club:** no en-
> trance charge, dream views, top
> cuisine at fair prices, centrally lo-
> cated near the tourist office – the
> Royal Yacht Club is the perfect
> spot to get a feel for Aqaba. Se-
> cure car parks are available be-
> tween the Ayla roundabout and
> the tourist office or right by the
> marina.

cheek-by-jowl. Still, neither water quality nor the coral reefs off the coast seem to be affected by this.

In the past, the container terminal used to be a more reliable source of income than tourism. In order for Aqaba not to be dependent on just one sector in the future, the ASEZA development agency has set up a whole bundle of projects: alongside numerous luxury resorts and five-star hotels, roads and apartments are being built. Over the coming years,

nian cities, for instance along the palm-fringed Corniche. Even in winter, Aqaba enjoys a mild spring climate; in summer however, it gets very hot. Average water temperatures hover around 23°C/73°F – ideal for snorkelling or diving.

SIGHTSEEING

AQABA MARINE PARK/AQUARIUM

The Aqaba Marine Park at South Beach 7km/4.5mi south of the city centre, at

Aqaba on the Red Sea is Jordan's only port and access to the sea

most of the container port is scheduled to be transferred south to the Saudi border. In order to bring young people into the city and stop emigration, several universities have been established here, amongst them a branch of the state-run University of Jordan and the private RSICA (Red Sea Institute for the Cinematic Arts).

Despite all this, Aqaba still has the character of a tranquil small town, which at night boasts more life than other Jorda-

the pier for the passenger ferry, holds attractions for all age groups. One highlight is birdwatching. The pretty aquarium yields exciting glimpses of the underwater world of the Red Sea – interesting for those who are neither into snorkelling nor diving. *Visitor centre daily 8am–5pm | tel. 03 2 03 58 01 and 03 2 03 58 03 | Aquarium Sat–Thu 8am–3.45pm, Fri 8am–5pm | admission 3 JD | Marine Park, in the Centre for Marine Research | www.aqaba.jo*

ARCHAEOLOGICAL MUSEUM

Behind the fort, the former residence of Sherif Hussein, great-grandfather of King Abdullah II, shows objects from the Islamic Middle Ages that were found in Ayla and Wadi Rum. *Daily April–Oct 8am–7pm, Nov–March 8am–4pm | Corniche | admission 1 JD*

AYLA

Remains of the Islamic city may be visited directly opposite the Mövenpick Hotel. In the daytime, the area is freely accessible. *Daily | Corniche | free admission*

FORT

In the fort built by the Mamluks in the 16th century, King Faisal set up camp after conquering Aqaba in 1917. The building was originally erected as a caravanserai for Egyptian Mecca pilgrims. At the southern end of the Corniche. *Daily 7.30am–7pm | free admission*

FOOD & DRINK

BLUE BAY ●

Delicious fish dishes, imaginative salads, laid-back ambience, friendly service – everything just comes together here. A tad more expensive than its rivals, but well worth it. An excellent after-dinner option is a trip to the ice-cream hatch of the Mövenpick Hotel. *Daily | As-Sadah Street | tel. 03 2 07 07 55 | Moderate*

INSIDER TIP CAPTAIN'S RESTAURANT

Excellent fish restaurant in the Captain's Hotel on a ☼ pretty terrace. Note that no alcohol is served here. *Daily | Corniche, Al-Nahda Street | tel. 03 2 016 905 and 03 2 06 07 10 | captains-jo.com | Moderate*

FLOKA

Very good fish restaurant with a terrace next to the Alcazar Hotel, where you may choose your own fish at the counter. *Daily | An-Nahda Street | tel. 03 2 016 636 | Moderate*

JAFRA AQABA

Down-to-earth Arab fare, shisha and Italian cappuccino. So cosy with its mix of rustic nostalgia and Pop Art. Traditional Arab breakfast with tea, thyme pizza and fresh-cheese specialities, traditional casseroles with yoghurt, Arabic bread and chickpeas. At night this turns into one of the hippest places for a shisha smoke. *Daily 8.30am–2am | Sa'adeh Street | tel. 079 7 50 00 41*

ROMERO

Italian, Japanese and oriental cuisine at the Royal Yacht Club. The ☼ terrace affords wonderful views of the harbour. *Daily | Royal Yacht Club, Corniche, tel. 03 2 02 24 64 | Expensive*

SHOPPING

To stock up on souvenirs and find good specialised stores head for Zahran Street, also called Post Office Street. Here, the *Redwan* bookshop has reading matter in English. Al Saadah Street (Pizza Street) too is a pretty shopping strip. The *Souk Ayadi* women's cooperative has a branch at the fort. The shopping centres sell Chinese mass-produced wares.

★ Coral Bay Hotel & Royal Diving Club

In Aqaba, the best spot for snorkellers is on this beach → p. 81

★ Wadi Rum

The quiet of the desert and Bedouin culture far from the trappings of modern civilisation → p. 83

MARCO POLO HIGHLIGHTS

SPORTS & ACTIVITIES

BOAT TOURS

Sindbad Cruises hires out the *Aladdin 24*, a trim, 30m/100ft INSIDER TIP wooden sailing boat that you can take for a tour through the bay. Or consider a motorboat day trip to *Pharaohs Island*. The crew will cook for you. *Sindbad Maritime Transportation | tel. 03 2 05 00 77 | www.sindbadjo.com*

INSIDER TIP JANNA SPA

The entire range of oriental health and beauty awaits you here. Particular plus points are the unassuming service and the affordable prices. Women only. *Sat–Thu 9am–9pm, Fri 12 noon–9pm | Al-Saadah St | reservations recommended | tel. 03 2 05 19 91 | www.janna-spa.com*

DIVING

Aqaba Adventure Divers: 5* PADI course. One of the best places to dive in Aqaba, 10km/6mi south above the road running along the sea. Accommodation can be provided, incl. full-board. Those who don't fancy diving can stretch out by the pool for 10 JD a day. *20 rooms | tel. 09 5 84 37 24 | www.aqaba-diving.com | Moderate*

Dive Aqaba: long-established club at the Qidra Hotel (see Where to Stay). One of the activities on offer is INSIDER TIP night diving with an underwater camera. *tel. 03 2 01 88 83 | www.diveaqaba.com*

Royal Diving Club: established diving club 17km/10mi south. You can dive straight in from the pontoon on the beach. *Southern Coastal Road | tel. 03 2 01 55 55 and 03 2 01 70 35 | www.rdc.jo*

Sea Star Watersports: some of the town's best diving instructors work from this club. *Al Saada Street | tel. 03 2 01 83 35 | www.aqabadivingseastar.com*

BEACHES

The ● popular beaches can be found south of the city centre. The visitor centre is located between sectors 3 and 4 (map at *www.aqaba.jo/en/node/1485*). Toilets, showers, changing rooms and permanent sunshades are free of charge. On Fridays and Saturdays it can get very busy. Many hotels and diving clubs offer access to their private beaches. Deckchair and towel are usually included in the price (from 8 JD per day), in the five-star hotels also a voucher for food and drink.

BARRACUDA DIVING CLUB ⚓

Popular diving club on the southern coast. International-standard training (PADI, BSAC) as well as individually tailored excursions where you may bring your own equipment. A shuttle bus runs from the centre of Aqaba, check the times beforehand. *Beach access with deck chair 8 JD per day, children 5 JD | tel. 03 2 06 05 01 | www.goaqabadive.com*

CORAL BAY HOTEL & ROYAL DIVING CLUB ⭐ ☀

A pontoon offers the best chance for snorkellers to enter water directly above coral reefs. Pretty beach, the only drawback being that you're not allowed to enter the water directly as the corals come up right to the shore. *Admission 10 JD, free for divers | 69 rooms | Southern Coastal Road | tel. 03 2 01 55 55 | www.rdc.jo | Expensive*

ENTERTAINMENT

INSIDER TIP ▶ 35° EAST GRILL BAR

Trendy location for night owls: food, cool beer, shisha, and hot dance parties. Thursday is disco night with a DJ spinning tunes, on other days salsa/Latin or karaoke. Pool table, live broadcasting of sports events. *Daily | Aqaba Gateway, 2nd floor | tel. 079 5 69 24 74 or 03 2 03 06 26*

ROVERS RETURN

Enjoy the wonderful night-time views across the bay on the ☀ terrace with a drink in your hand. *Daily | in the Gateway at the Ayla Circle | tel. 03 2 03 20 30 | www.roversreturnjordan.com*

WHERE TO STAY

The seaside is dominated by five-star hotels with their private beaches. The cheaper hotels are in the town. Some have shuttle buses to ferry their guests to the beaches in the south.

INSIDER TIP ▶ AL QIDRA HOTEL AQABA

Very clean, good beds, friendly staff. Quiet and central, and air-conditioned rooms (up to five beds). Diving courses can be arranged through the hotel. *32 rooms | Al-Saadah Street | tel. 03 2 01 42 30 and 03 2 02 25 55 | www.alqidrahotelaqaba.com | Moderate*

BEDOUIN MOON VILLAGE ☀

Generously sized, quiet cottage village near the beach, for independent travellers and families, approx. 12km/7mi outside the town centre. Simply furnished, clean chalets with air-conditioning,

Beach life on the Red Sea in Aqaba provides relaxation after all that culture and sightseeing

restaurant, a large pool, a Bedouin-community tent with sea view, snorkel equipment hire. The owners organise tours to Wadi Rum and Petra. *12 chalets with bath, of which 3 single rooms, 5 doubles, 4 chalets sleeping 5–8 people, 2 doubles with shared bathroom | Southern Coastal Road | tel. 03 2 01 55 25, mobile 079 5 38 19 79 | www.bedouinmoon village.com | Moderate*

CAPTAIN'S HOTEL

Solid mid-range hotel in the town centre. Nicely furnished bright en-suite rooms with TV. Elevator, car park, knowledgeable staff, fair prices. The owners also run a restaurant and desert camp in Wadi Rum. *64 rooms | Nahda Street | tel. 03 2 06 07 10 | www.captains-jo.com | Moderate*

LOW BUDGET

▶ South of the centre of Aqaba ☼ (116 B5) (*Ⓜ A13*) you can swim for free and use the sunshades, changing rooms and showers (bring flip-flops). You'll recognise it by an old wooden boat converted into a café.

▶ Consider buying small electrical appliances in Aqaba (116 B5) (*Ⓜ A13*). In the duty-free zone many articles are up to 20 per cent cheaper than elsewhere.

▶ Between 6am and 6pm, blue mini buses (look for the yellow sign: 'South Beach') will take you from the Mamluk fort in Aqaba (116 B5) (*Ⓜ A13*) to the southern beach – for 1 JD.

KEMPINSKI AQABA

The most recent addition to the five-star establishments in the town centre. Splendid views of the Gulf of Aqaba and Sinai. A good choice for travellers without children and businesspeople. *200 rooms | King Hussein Street | tel. 03 2 09 08 88 | www.kempinski.com/en/ aqaba | Expensive*

MÖVENPICK RESORT & SPA TALA BAY

Relatively new hotel complex right on the Red Sea, a good choice for families and sports fans. Extensive complex styled with taste, including landscaped water features and spa treatments, a 150m/150yd hotel beach with private coral reef, diving school, gym and entertainment for children. Italian and Arab cuisine; the open-air lounge on the sea provides shishas and cocktails in the daytime, and bellydancing in the evenings. Dance bar open till 3 in the morning. *306 rooms, of which 145 family rooms sleeping up to 5 | tel. 03 2 09 03 00 | www. moevenpick-hotels.com | Expensive*

INSIDER TIP MY HOTEL

Mid-range hotel with large pool and restaurant, and a central location (next to the Floka Restaurant, near the Jett bus station). A little sterile, but clean and comfortable, with friendly staff. Guests may use the beach of the nearby Interconti Hotel for 15 JD a day. *63 rooms, of which 5 suites and 2 family rooms | Al-Nahda Street | tel. 03 2 03 08 90 | www. myhotel-jordan.com | Moderate*

RADISSON BLUE TALA BAY RESORT

Non-residents may use the beach and pool for 30 JD, which includes a 20 JD food-and-drink voucher. *336 rooms | tel. 03 2 09 07 77 | info.talabay.aqaba@ radissonblu.com | Expensive*

RAED HOTEL SUITES

Central, quiet, clean, friendly management. The rooms sleep between one to five people, some (fourth floor) offer sea views and/or balcony. The rooms have tiled floors, air-conditioning, and a fridge. Satellite TV, free Wi-Fi. *57 rooms | Saada Street | 03 2 018686 | www.raedhotel.com | Moderate*

INFORMATION

Tourist Information Centre | daily 8am–6pm | Al-Hammamat Al-Tunisiyya Street | tel. 03 2 03 53 60 | www.aqaba.jo

WADI RUM

(116 C4–5) (*∅ B–C 12–13*) ★ **'Vast, echoing and godlike' – these were the words that Lawrence of Arabia used to describe this desert landscape.**

The rock formations thrown upwards thirty million years ago from deeper geological layers now jut out of the earth like columns or pillars. The rock formation to the left in front of the new visitor centre is also called 'The Seven Pillars of Wisdom' after T E Lawrence's autobiography. The extreme erosion caused by the major differences in temperature between day and night has furrowed the range further and opened it up into fantastical shapes.

Wadi Rum belongs to the territory of the Howeitat tribe, with some of the Howeitat living in the village of *Rum*. Lately the central government has been trying to increase its slice of the money earned from the tourists visiting Wadi Rum. Thus the first thing visitors see, some 6km/4mi before getting to the village, is a huge car park. At the visitor centre, travellers book a fixed tour and are assigned a Bedouin as a guide. As the inhabitants of Wadi Rum don't want rival guides from neighbouring *Disi* to work in their area, various zones have been created. Make sure to choose a tour beginning in Rum, which is particularly scenic. In order to guarantee this, put the Nabataean temple onto your wish list. In any case try and spend one night in Wadi Rum in a Bedouin tent. Sunset and the star-studded sky are veritable treats.

In the rocky gorges of Wadi Rum, jeeps are a main means of transport

WADI RUM

SIGHTSEEING

AIN SHELAALI (LAWRENCE SPRING)
Apart from the Nabatean inscriptions, the place is not much to write home about. But if you are prepared to climb a bit, you'll be rewarded with ☆ fine views across Wadi Shelaali.

BURDAH ROCK BRIDGE
Deep in the wadi, hidden away, this natural rock bridge has formed at a height of approx. 80m/260ft. The courageous climb up and have their picture taken; be warned, however, that this is not without risk.

SMALL SIQ
Narrow rock gorge with natural water basin. *Jabal Khazali*

LAWRENCE HOUSE
A pile of rocks serves as a reminder of the place where T.E. Lawrence spent the night. The nearby red sand dune is worth a detour.

NABATEAN TEMPLE
Approx. 500m/500yd beyond the village at the entrance to Wadi Rum, the remains of a Nabataean temple (1st century) are visible; it was later expanded by the Romans.

INSIDER TIP ORYX ENCLOSURE
This enclosure gives visitors the chance to admire white oryx antelopes, which were nearly hunted to extinction. In 2002 a small herd of these sabre antelopes was once again settled here.

UMM FROUTH
The so-called Small Bridge is just as suitable for pictures as the Burdah Rock Bridge. As this rock arch rises only about 20m/65ft above the ground, it's easier to climb. If you suffer from vertigo, it's still probably not a good idea.

FOOD & DRINK

The visitor centre has a very good, air-conditioned if not exactly cheap restaurant: the Wadi Rum Gate Restaurant *(daily | tel. 03 2 06 07 10 | Moderate)*. There are other, smaller places to choose from too. The best option really is to have Bedouin cook for you in the tent.

SPORTS & ACTIVITIES

BALLOON TRIPS ●
The Royal Aero Sports Club of Jordan offers professionally guided hot-air balloon trips. Dates and hours are agreed on an individual basis and dependent on weather conditions. Duration incl. transport in Wadi Rum approx. 3 hrs. *tel. 079 8 70 66 22 | www.royalaerosports.com*

CLIMBING
If you want to go climbing, take one of the local guides; check with the visitor centre or contact: *Attayak Aouda, mobile phone 079 5 83 47 36, attayak@rum guides.com | Attayak Ali, mobile phone 079 5 89 97 23, info@bedouinroads. com | Saleem Ali, mobile 079 6 48 28 01, saleemali@jordantracks.com | Attayak Zalabiya, mobile phone 079 5 60 96 91*

HORSERIDING
The only place where you can hire a horse lies some 200m/200yd to the right of the road into Wadi Rum, before the crossroads after Disi. Hacks and day treks, also with overnight stays. *Atallah Sweilhin | tel. 03 2 03 35 08,*

BEDOUIN TOUR
It is possible to organise your stay with a Bedouin direct. Send an email in English

In Wadi Rum, adventurous travellers will find fine climbing routes in the red rock

at least 48 hours before your intended visit, so he can obtain the authorities' permission. This is worth your while if you'd like to stay in a particular Bedouin camp. The ☼ INSIDER TIP *Camp of Zidane Al-Zalabieh (tel. 03 2 03 41 77 | zedn_a@yahoo. com)* boasts one of the most beautiful locations; the man himself will occasionally recite Islamic poetry. Just a few miles further along, his brother *Eid* has his camp *(tel. 03 2 03 53 21, eidsabah@yahoo.com)*. The brothers can arrange an exciting tour to *Wadi Sabet* (also *Tariq Abu Gaspard*). From the ☼ mountain you have a panoramic view all the way to the Saudi hills. A narrow gorge runs along the valley.

WHERE TO STAY

OVERNIGHT STAY IN A BEDOUIN TENT

Spend your night at Wadi Rum in a Bedouin tent in the desert *(with dinner and breakfast 35 JD per person)*. The arrangements can be made at the visitor centre. For hygienic reasons, bring your own covers for pillows and bed. In winter a sleeping bag is handy. At Disi, Bedouin camps with electric light and disco have been set up; that is not where you'll ex-

actly experience the quiet of the desert. A fine choice is the INSIDER TIP *Captains Desert Camp (tel. 03 2 0169 05 | www. captains-jo.com)*. The ● *Bait Ali Camp* too offers desert feeling with tent accommodation in comfort. Desert trips by jeep or quad, riding tours or hot air balloon trips *(mobile phone 079 5 54 81 33 and 077 7 54 81 33 | www.baitali.com)*.

CAMPSITE AT THE RESTHOUSE

The only accommodation option in Rum is the campsite at the Resthouse. The two-person tents occupy a less-than-romantic position right next to the car park. *30 tents, each sleeping 2 | tel. 03 2 018867 | Budget*

INFORMATION

Visitor centre at the entrance to Wadi Rum | daily 8am–7pm | tel. 03 2 09 06 00 | admission 5 JD | taking your own car 20–35 JD per day | 4WD car with guide (for up to six people): for half a day 70 JD, for the entire day with complete programme of visits 80 JD | half-day camel ride 25 JD

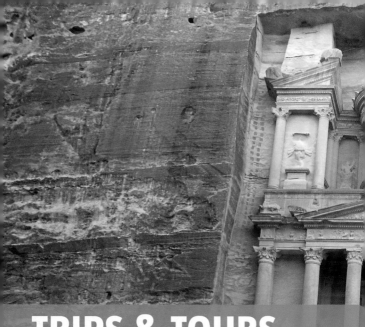

TRIPS & TOURS

The tours are marked in green in the road atlas,
the pull-out map and on the back cover

1 ON THE BIBLE TRAIL

In Jordan the Bible can serve as a travel guide too. The Old and New Testaments name some 100 places that lie in today's Hashemite kingdom. The names of the prophets as well as other fathers of the monotheistic religions are intricately connected with the landscape east of the Jordan River. Visitors can walk in the footsteps of the founders of Judaism and Christianity along the Jordan Rift Valley, on the heights above the Dead Sea and into Wadi Araba. A tour taking in the most important sites can be done from Amman in a day (150km/95mi).

The **baptism site of Jesus → p. 59** (Arabic: *Al-Maghtas)* in the Jordan Valley is the starting point for this tour though the Holy Land. From Amman you can reach this large area in some 40 minutes by car (50km/30mi): head towards the Dead Sea until you cannot drive straight any further. To your left lies the **Dead Sea → p. 60,** to your right is the way to the baptism site. This is the supposed location of Bethany, the place where John the Baptist lived and baptised Jesus ('Bethany beyond the Jordan, where John was baptising', John 1:28). Jesus is said to have returned to this place years later, as is written in St John's Gospel 10:40: '... and went away again beyond Jordan to the place where John at first baptised, and there he abode.' The place has held a sacred character since the 9th century BC, when the prophet Elijah lived

Tours of Jordan – experience biblical sites, the historic region of Balqa, the more recent Amman and rare natural wonders

here. The Bible tells how Elijah divided the waters of the Jordan and crossed the river with his successor, the prophet Elisha, without getting his feet wet, before ascending to heaven from a low hill which is known as **Elija's Hill** and forms the heart of Bethany: '... there appeared a chariot of fire and horses of fire ... and Elijah went up by a whirlwind into heaven' (Second Book of Kings 2:5–14).
If you'd like to take a break after the visit (which takes about two hours), why not head for **Amman Beach** → p. 63, south of the luxury hotels, for a dip in the Dead Sea? Otherwise drive back a few miles on the road to Amman, before turning right at the village of Kufrein in the direction of Madaba. The road wends its way up beautifully to ☀ **Mount Nebo** → p. 70. This is where Moses is supposed to have seen the Promised Land following the Exodus from Egypt (Fifth Book of Moses 34). He is said to be buried 'opposite Beth-Peor' (Fifth Book of Moses 34:6): The place formerly called **Beth-Peor** lies east of Mount Nebo near the Moses

Springs, yet the location of Moses' grave is not known.

A few miles further on, the Christian town of **Madaba** → p. 68 features numerous churches. This is also where you'll find the oldest map of the region as a mosaic in **St George's Church** → p. 69. The traditional restaurant of **Haret Jdouna** → p. 70 in the same street makes a good rest stop.

dias convinced her daughter Salome to ask for John's head. John was decapitated, and Salome brought her mother the head on a platter (St Mark's Gospel 6:14 to 6:29). Today, Mukawir has only a few ⚜ **foundations of the Machaerus Fort**, but the views are enchanting. By the way: the only place where original Jordanian carpets are woven is here in Mukawir.

Ancient panoramic map: the famous mosaic of Palestine in Madaba

Taking the **King's Highway** → p. 64 going south you're on one of the world's oldest routes. 12km/7.5mi south of Madaba turn right for **Mukawir**. Machaerus, as the place was once known, held a fortified **mountain castle of King Herod Antipas** → p. 71. When John the Baptist publicly reproached the king for his unlawful relationship with his sister-in-law Herodias, Herod had him imprisoned. Hero-

On your way back to Madaba or Amman you might want to take in Libb and enjoy the idyllic agricultural landscape.

STROLL THROUGH THE JABAL AMMAN RESIDENTIAL QUARTER
A two-hour walk (with breaks) through this neighbourhood of Amman, at the end of

Rainbow Street going east from the 1st Circle, provides an excellent introduction to Jordan's more recent history. An earthquake in 1927 destroyed many of the houses built by Circassian immigrants. This was where the elite of the newly created Emirate of Transjordan built their residences under King Talal, the father of King Hussein, who died in 1999. However, many of the houses of architectural interest stand empty and have been left to decay.

On the right-hand side of Rainbow Street (a good half-mile counting from the 1st Circle), at the corner of Rifahat at-Tahtawi Street, you can spot the modest INSIDERTIP birthplace of King Hussein. His brother, long-term Crown Prince Hassan, was born here too. Devoid of ornamentation, the grey building with green balconies is a reminder of the royal family's humble beginnings. Some of the older residents still remember Hussein's early childhood and adolescence, which were spent here.

Crossing Rainbow Street and entering Fawzy al-Maalouf Street to the left, you'll first find on the left-hand side the Jordan River Foundation → p. 39, in a house belonging to the Christian Qussus family. This was also the residence of the British representative in Transjordan, Alec Kirkbride. 50m/50yd further along, still on the left-hand side you'll see the House of the Bilbaysi Family, built from white stone, and next to it, the family's pink-and-white limestone palace. Ismael Bilbaysi was an Egyptian immigrant who rose from construction worker to pasha. Guests of the royal family were accommodated in the palace, when the original royal palace became too small. A resident's association organises the INSIDERTIP Souk Jara flea market (Fri 10am–4pm), where you can buy 🌿 green products as well as freshly

squeezed fruit juices and homemade cake. At the end of the street, a small set of steps leads to the 🍴 Café Wild Jordan → p. 37, where you can enjoy the view with a tea on the terrace.

Now return to Fawzy al-Maalouf Street. The Ahliyya School opposite was founded by British missionaries in 1926. Plot no. 40 is surrounded by high walls. This was the residence of British officer Glubb Pasha, leader of the Arab Legion in the 1930s. At the end head left along Omar Bin al-Khattab Street, until you hit Books@Café → p. 37 on the left. The first-floor 🍴 terrace affords far-reaching views of the eastern part of Amman.

3 THE DISCOVERERS' ROUTE: CHARMING HILLS AND HISTORIC TOWNS

After spending some days in Amman, are your eyes craving for some green? Take a day trip into the nearby Balqa region, to visit the villages of Iraq Al Amir and Fuheis as well as the former capital, Salt. You will be surprised how quickly you can reach nature from the urban desert and discover all there is to see.

From Amman → p. 32 take the continuation of Zahran Street via the 8th Circle in the direction of Wadi as-Sir. You might like to have breakfast at the small river and take a look at the remains of Roman aqueducts. In spring, you might spot a black iris, the Jordanian national flower, in the meadows.

Some 10km/6mi past Wadi as-Sir you reach the village of INSIDERTIP Iraq al-Amir ('Cave of the Prince'), housing the craft workshops of the Jordan River Foundation. Opposite, about a dozen caves have been carved into the rock, and are reached by steep steps. Inside the caves there are two Aramaic inscriptions. One inscription outside (on the last cave to the right when you're standing in front of it) names the Jewish Tobiades family, who are said to have lived here in the 2nd century BC.

A little further along, on the left-hand side a narrow road leads to the **Qasr al-Abd** (Slaves' Castle). Built in the 2nd century BC, this monument represents one of the few well-preserved ruins from the Hellenistic era. The stone blocks, each weighing up to 20 tons, are as impressive as the one remaining stone lion and the friezes, partly lying on the ground. Ask the guard to show you the museum for a 2–3 JD tip and also the slideshow if you can – it's worth it.

Drive along picturesque Wadi Shu'aib via Wadi as-Sir to **Fuheis**. In the Al Balad part of town, you'll find a dozen or so craftsmen's studios along Rowaq Al Balqa Street. A good place to take a pit stop after a short stroll is the beautiful Zuwwadeh restaurant-café.

Carry on driving into ● **Salt** (from the Greek 'Saltos', forest), once the cultural and political centre of the country, where it is usually cooler. It was in Salt that in 1921 the foundation of the state of Jordan was proclaimed. Start your tour at the **Archaeological Museum** *(Deir Street (Prince Hamza Street) | April–Oct Sat–Thu 8am–4pm, Nov–March Sat–Thu 8am–5pm | admission 2 JD)* – the exhibition is small, but it's fun exploring the nooks and crannies of this 19th-century building. Afterwards take a stroll through the small Arab souk in Hammamat Street. At the end of the street, on the left-hand side you'll find the **City Museum** *(Wadi Al Akrad Street | Sun–Thu 8am–3pm | admission 1JD)*, the Ottoman residence of the Jaber family, where the architecture mixes Italian and oriental styles. After a short wander around here, cross the square and follow the marked

INSIDER TIP **Heritage Trail**, up the stairs to the right of the mosque. After leading to various sights this trail will take you back into the city centre. Most of the cafés and restaurants in Salt are not yet geared up for tourists. If you have transport, use the opportunity and drive the 15km/9mi out to the **Mountain Breeze Country Club → p. 59**, which dishes up very tasty food amidst the greenery, and serves alcoholic drinks too. From here, the drive back into the centre of Amman takes roughly 45 minutes.

4 FERNS AND FISH: INSIDE THE CANYON PARADISE OF WADI IBN HAMMAD

The ● **Wadi Ibn Hammad** canyon near Karak is not only worth visiting for its lush, near-tropical vegetation. It also has the advantage that even beginners with medium fitness levels may hike it without problems. The most beautiful part is the first 1,5 hours of walking (not including breaks). The trail is easy to find, the gradient manageable, and fun virtually guaranteed. Be prepared to get your feet wet though.

Before you set off: while the water in Wadi Ibn Hammad is usually not deep, make sure to stow your camera, mobile phone and documents in watertight containers. To be on the safe side, deposit towels and a change of clothes in the car. Make sure you take enough drinking water and something to cover your head. Do not hike on your own! *For further hiking tips for independent travellers see p. 94.*

Getting there: there is no direct bus connection. On the old King's Highway (35), a little over 7km/4mi north of **Karak → p. 67** turn off west in the direction of Batir (signposted). Past Batir, follow the road leading down the mountain, for 2km/1.25mi to the T-junction, where you turn left. From here you can already get an overview of the Wadi Ibn Hammad. In spring, the flowers are just overwhelming in their beauty. After under a

and back again, is nearly as beautiful. When walking through the Siq, watch out for rare animals (small brown Blanford foxes, the Jordanian garra fish) and the brightly coloured rocks that owe their shades to minerals. After a walk of

Wet feet down below, bright luminous colours above in Wadi Ibn Hammad

mile you will see a sign. After that drive for approx. 7.5km/4.5mi on a narrow, winding yet well-maintained road down to the hot springs. Once you see a natural pool on the other bank, amidst palms, oleander shrubs, ferns and mosses, park your car.

The hike leads along the edge of the river bed and sometimes right through it. In theory you could cross the entire canyon to the Dead Sea or the Dead Sea Highway without climbing gear (length: a little over 10km/6mi or 12km/7.5mi). However, the short version, where you hike for 3–6km/2–3.5mi into the canyon

around 1.5 hours the Siq ends and the river bed broadens, leaving hardly any shade. Take a shower under the waterfall on the right, cool off and rest awhile before heading back or carry on for another hour before you reach another waterfall. From there it'll take you just under three hours to get back to where you started out.

Careful: desert riverbeds (wadis) are prone to occasional violent and extreme flooding. In winter and in the rainy season, whatever you do stick to trails above the river bed proper or just forego wadi treks.

SPORTS & ACTIVITIES

Diving and snorkelling on the coral reefs of the Red Sea near Aqaba is one of the main attractions for active holidaymakers. Water temperatures of 23°C/73°F on average offer ideal conditions for exploring the colourful underwater fauna and flora. The coral reefs of the Red Sea are amongst the most beautiful on the planet. However, hikers too find an increasing amount of reliable infrastructure in the nature reserves: accommodation right in the heart of nature, hiking trails and trained guides.

CYCLING

No cycle paths, reckless drivers, extreme ascents: if you still want to bike in Jordan, you'll need a good level of fitness and strong nerves. Still, ever more Jordanians are discovering the advantages of a bike, and there is some infrastructure for tourists too. In the flat wetland habitat of Azraq, the *Azraq Lodge* hires out bikes and offers tours. If you'd like to go in for some sporty biking during your stay: Amman bike-shop owner and activist Sari Husseini organises **INSIDER TIP** a tour every Friday. Contact through *www.cycling-jordan.com*, the *Cycling Jordan* facebook group or *tel. 078 5 55 25 25*. Another fine event is the annual women's peace bike tour 'Follow the Women' (more information from *sara@globalone.com.jo*)

DIVING

⭐ In *Aqaba*, several diving clubs offer

Whether coral reefs or canyon landscapes – adventurous visitors to Jordan will find plenty of exciting spots

equipment and classes. While the *Royal Diving Club* boasts some coral reefs right in front of the beach, other diving schools take divers by boat to spots stretching along the coast to the Saudi border. As special treats there are a Russian tank and a Lebanese freighter that were sunk for wreck divers. Another recommendation is a day trip to *Pharaohs Island,* in Egyptian waters, where the diving is particularly fine. All diving schools run diving courses accredited with the internationally valid PADI system. Theo-

retical and practical exams can be taken here too. The complete gear, from diving suit and flippers all the way to oxygen flasks, can be rented, including gear for children.

GOLF

Golfers will find a special treat here in this desert country – as long as they're up for playing on sand and rock for once. In which case they have to spread a small mat of artificial lawn for tee-off. They'll need it on the country's only golf course, the *Bisharat Golf Club* south of Amman. There are no ditches or ponds, but there is a club house with a large terrace. The available nine holes can be connected up to form a 18-hole course. *Bisharat Golf Club | Airport Road | 15km/9mi south of Amman, exit at Choueifat School, turn right behind the school and continue to the club entrance | tel. 079 5 52 03 34.*

With its varied rock landscapes and favourable climate, Jordan is an attractive destination for hikers and climbers. The country's nature reserves are run by the Royal Society for the Conservation of Nature (RSCN), with plenty of well-marked hiking and climbing routes. At the *Ajloun Nature Reserve* some 80km/50mi north of Amman you can expect rolling Mediterranean hilly landscapes with oaks, pines and the red-barked wild strawberry tree. In *Azraq* you can do a spot of exotic birdwatching. In *Dana*, *Petra* and *Wadi Rum* you'll be trekking through exciting canyons and across colourful rock formations. In terms of difficulty, everything from a simple stroll to demanding treks or tours including climbing spots (*Dana*) is available. Demanding canyoning, with abseiling and swimming (*Wadi Mujib*) all the way to freeclimbing (*Wadi Rum*), is also possible. In some places trained RSCN guides are obligatory. For climbing tours in *Wadi Rum* see the chapter South. Tours and tips for independent hikes can be found in the book *Walks, Treks, Caves, Climbs & Canyons* by Di Taylor and Tony Howard (order online) as well as online at *www.desertguides.net*. The book *Treks & Climbs in Wadi Rum* by Tony Howard lists numerous climbing tours.

The Royal Society for the Conservation of Nature mainly operates standard hiking tours for groups and also offers accommodation in the protected areas. For information and bookings see *www.rscn. org.jo,* and click yourself through to *Wild Jordan.* Both standard tours and tailor-made tours can be booked through the Terhaal company, *www.terhaal.com.*

There are also facilities for indoor climbing: the country's first professional climbing hall has been opened in Marj Hammam, a southwestern suburb of Amman. You can book climbing lessons at short notice here, but do make a telephone reservation to be on the safe side. Climb-

SAFE HIKING AND CLIMBING

▶ Find out in advance whether you need permission from the RSCN for the route you want to explore (e. g. Wadi Mujib)

▶ There is no mountain rescue, and many routes are not supervised. Never hike alone, and take precautions in case somebody needs to come and look for you. Tell somebody where you are heading and when you will be back

▶ Take a fully charged mobile phone even if many canyons have no network coverage

▶ Minimum provisions: two litres of drinking water, head covering, spray plaster

▶ Wear sturdy ankle-high boots and airy clothing

Fast, loud and trendy: jet-skiing in the waters of Aqaba

ing gear – including for children – may be brought along or hired. *Daily 10am–10pm | getting there: Amman 8th circle in the direction of the airport, onwards in the direction of the Dead Sea, signposted from Marj Hammam | tel. 06 5 73 61 77 | www.climbat.com*

HORSERIDING

The best place to ride out on horseback is sandy *Wadi Rum* with endless spaces that just ask to be explored at a gallop. Day tours, including overnight stays, if required, can be organised through *Atallah Sweilhin | tel. 03 2 03 35 08 | stables at the access road to Wadi Rum*, or *Jordantracks | Saleem Ali, | tel. 079 6 48 28 01 | www.jordantracks.com*

The areas around *Petra* and *Wadi Mussa* too take on a new and fascinating dimension if explored on horseback. One of the companies offering trips like this is *La Beduina Eco Tours (tel. 03 2 15 70 99 | www.labeduinatours.com).*

WATER SKIING & SCOOTERS

The large hotels in *Aqaba* with direct access to the water (Mövenpick, Aquamarina I, Intercontinental) offer various water sports – including water skiing and scooters. So far, there is no culture of windsurfing, possibly because windsurfers could too easily cross the border to Israel, which runs in the waters of the Gulf.

TRAVEL WITH KIDS

Jordan is an ideal holiday destination for families with children. The dry climate throughout (with the exception of the Jordan Valley) can be handled even by small babies without any problems. Not least, many public toilets are equipped with changing facilities.

While Jordan still has relatively few attractions specially geared towards children, young holiday guests will be pampered all round. Numerous activities such as circus, theatre and music are on offer at the *Summer Arts Festival* in Amman *(July/August | www.calendar.jo and www.visit jordan.com)*.

In the larger cities – Amman, Zarqa, Aqaba, Irbid – new parks and playgrounds have been established, though they aren't always that easy to find (just ask Jordanian families in the street). In the summer holidays, there are occasional dodgems, carousels and bouncy castles. Make sure you check for loose parts, sharp edges and other danger spots.

The nature reserves are interesting for children too; kids as young as four can be brought on hikes. Sturdy footwear is important, as is light-coloured headgear and lightweight, long-sleeved clothing in light colours for additional protection against the sun. And a night in the Bedouin tent, in Wadi Rum for instance, makes for an unforgettable experience.

AMMAN

AMMAN WAVES (112 C5) (*𝔐 D5*)

Large leisure waterpark with many shady spots. The restaurants are relatively expensive, so bringing a picnic pays off. *April–Sept daily 10am–7pm | admission 15 JD, children 10 JD | from the 7th Circle in the direction of the airport, signposted on right-hand side after approx. 12km/7.5mi | www.ammanwaves.com*

GÉRARD ICE-CREAM

Top for everything sweet in Amman: fabulous ice-cream, cakes and biscuits. *Several branches, amongst them: Abdoun Circle (U A6) (𝔐 a6), at the Automobile Museum (112 C5) (𝔐 D5), in the City Mall (112 C5) (𝔐 D5)*

INSIDER TIP CHILDREN'S MUSEUM ☀ (112 C5) (*𝔐 D5*)

Romp around and learn! Discover workshops, music concerts and theatre performances. *Sat–Thu 9am–6pm, Fri 10am–7pm | King Hussein Park, exit off King Abdullah II Street (next to the Automobile Museum) | www.cmj.jo*

Playing around in the water, discovering nature and the reward of a fortifying biscuit afterwards – little guests are welcome everywhere

PLAYGROUND AT HUSSEIN PARK ☀
(112 C5) (*ᎀ D5*)

Hussein Park (in the south, entrance opposite City Mall) has a sandpit with decent equipment (little shade, restaurant nearby).

SPORTS CITY (U B1) (*ᎀ b1*)

Well cared-for large open-air swimming complex with three pools (of which two are suitable for non-swimmers), water garden, slide and a paddling pool for toddlers. Guests are allowed to bring food and drink, but the snack bars also sell fries, burgers or salad. *Daily 6.30am–5.45pm | outside area 25 May–30 Sept, admission 15 JD, interior area 1 Oct–24 May, admission 10 JD | at Sports City roundabout, entrance from Shaheed Street, in the direction of the tennis court*

THE SOUTH

INSIDER TIP **BEDOUIN POLICE**

At Wadi Rum (116 C5) (*ᎀ B13*) near the *Resthouse* you'll find the Bedouin police

station, camels and all: always a hit with the children.

MÖVENPICK AQABA (116 B5) (*ᎀ A13*)

Next to the hotel entrance, the German Bakery serves ice-cream, cakes and muffins, the way kids like them. You could eat from the floor it's so clean. Either go for a takeaway or enjoy a break with shady seating and water features. *Daily 8am–9pm | Corniche*

NEPTUNE (116 B5) (*ᎀ A13*)

From Aqaba take a INSIDER TIP tour on the Neptune. This pleasure boat has a glass bottom, so even non-swimmers and non-divers may experience the depths of the Gulf. *Tour (approx. 1 hr) 18 JD, with beach access 24 JD | Tala Bay | tel. 077 9 43 09 69 | www.aqababoat.com*

PLAYGROUND (116 B5) (*ᎀ A13*)

Between the Ayla roundabout and the Mamluk Fort in Aqaba you'll find a well-equipped playground with plenty of shade.

FESTIVALS & EVENTS

Workers in Jordan don't really enjoy regulated holidays – it is the numerous official holidays that ensure they get their due rest. For *Eid al-Fitr* at the end of *Ramadan* (the month of fasting) in particular, and for the *Eid al-Adha* Festival of Sacrifice, which lasts several days, the locals drive to the shores of the Red Sea or Dead Sea. As hotels and restaurants are full to breaking point at that time, tourists should try and avoid visiting during those times.

Nor is Ramadan the best time to visit Jordan really. Many restaurants close for the entire month, and opening times are reduced. In the large hotels and tourist facilities it's business as usual. Between September and Mai several cultural weeks and festivals take place in Amman. The highlight is the *Jordan Festival* with high-calibre concerts and art exhibitions staged in Amman, Jerash and Petra, as well as at the Dead Sea.

PUBLIC HOLIDAYS

1 Jan *New Year;* **30 Jan** *Birthday of King Abdullah II;* **1 May** *Labour Day;* **25 May** *Independence Day;* **14 Nov** *Birthday of King Hussein;* **25 Dec** *Christmas*

RELIGIOUS HOLIDAYS

Every year, the date of the religious holidays shifts backwards in relation to the global (western) calculation by approx. ten to eleven days, as they are calculated following the lunar calendar. The dates may also differ from the ones given here by one to two days, as their beginning at New Moon is determined by the naked eye.

▶ *Ramadan:* Islamic month of fasting where nothing should be eaten or drunk between sunrise and sundown. Start: 9 July 2013, 28 June 2014

▶ *Eid al-Fitr:* three to four-day festival marking the end of Ramadan. Start: 8 Aug 2013, 28 July 2014

▶ *Eid al-Adha:* four-day Festival of Sacrifice commemorating Abraham's willingness to make sacrifice. Any Muslim who can afford to do so should kill a sheep and share it with the needy. Start: 25 Oct 2012, 15 Oct 2013, 4 Oct 2014

▶ *Moulid al-Nabi (Prophet's Birthday):* 23/24 Jan 2013, 12/13 Jan 2014

▶ *1st Muharram (Islamic New Year):* 15 Nov 2012, 4 Nov 2013, 25 Oct 2014

Plenty of religious holidays, a vintage car rally and many arts festivals – celebrate them all with the Jordanians

FESTIVALS AND EVENTS

MARCH/APRIL

▶ Amman International Theatre Festival. *aitf@nol.com.jo*

APRIL

▶ *Dead Sea Marathon:* Whether the ultra, regular or half-marathon version: this run is sure to be an experience. The *Amman Road Runners* have been organising this mega sports event since 1993. In December another marathon is run in Aqaba. *www.deadseamarathon.com*

MAY

▶ *International Dance Festival:* taking place at various places around Jordan. *zakharefinmotion.blogspot.com*
▶ *The Jewel that is Jordan:* every other or every third year, this rally features spectacular vintage cars. Routes vary. *www.thejewelevents.com*

JULY

▶ INSIDER TIP *Fuheis Festival:* Good-vibe cultural festival around the village of Fuheis (half an hour from Amman). In early July this Christian village puts on entertainment deep into the night: open-air stages with theatre and music, and numerous art galleries stay open until late. *tel. 077 7 42 46 76 | www.fuheis.net*

JULY/AUGUST

▶ *Jerash Festival:* for decades the ● most important cultural event in Jordan, the festival has been revived, following an enforced break lasting several years. International artists share the stage with their Arab counterparts. One highlight is the performance of the Royal Jordanian Marching Band. *www.calendar.jo*
▶ ★ *Jordan Festival:* a month of concerts featuring international and Arab artists, dance, readings, performances in various towns and regions. *Friends Of Jordan Festival | tel. 06 46 13 30 0 | www. visitjordan.com/jordanfestival*

LINKS, BLOGS, APPS & MORE

LINKS

▶ www.guide2jordan.com Online portal with current and practical information covering all kinds of aspects, including news

▶ www.nomadstravel.co.uk Webpage of Di Taylor and Tony Howard, pioneers of hiking and climbing in Jordan and authors of the *Jordan – Walks, Treks, Caves, Climbs and Canyons* hiking guide

▶ www.ammansnob.com Online portal with plenty of addresses and practical information on Amman and Aqaba (also on facebook and twitter)

▶ www.liveinaqaba.com Online portal with practical information on Aqaba: restaurants, shopping, spas, leisure

BLOGS & FORUMS

▶ www.jordanjubilee.com The best travel blog on Jordan by a long way, with plenty of information on the land and its people. By Ruth Caswell, who has been living here for over 20 years (also available in book form)

▶ www.black-iris.com This blog by political scientist and IT expert Nassim Tarawneh is the best introduction to the independent Jordanian blogosphere

▶ www.360east.com Commentaries on current developments in society and politics, as well as IT-related advice

▶ http://forum.virtualtourist.com/forum-2964-1-Travel-Jordan-1-forum.html Forum with many practical tips by other travellers and locals

VIDEOS

▶ http://www.youtube.com/watch?v=VAXu4ODpqmk A few minutes of jaw-dropping images from Petra, set to music

▶ feed://www.peacecorps.gov/wws/multimedia/language/arabic.xml Arabic lessons for beginners: day-to-day phrases (saying hello, numbers, how to ask questions, etc.) as spoken in

Jordan. While you might not be able to drive a hard bargain after studying this, it will open up conversations

▶ http://www.youtube.com/watch?v=S9X3pIX7UoU Interview with Queen Rania on a US chat show, showing off her beauty, poise and social cred to maximum effect

▶ http://www.youtube.com/user/Terhaaladventure Images and videos of hotspots for active holidaymakers in Jordan: nature, canyoning, desert adventures, to a background of Arab music

▶ http://www.youtube.com/playlist?list=PL3A36E6DE4F646E9E Sounds of Jordan. A musical playlist

▶ Jordan: Rough Guides Sights, restaurants, shopping, weather, travelling inside the country. In English for Nokia, but also available for iPhone and iPad

▶ Animals of Jordan Well-structured app with detailed information on animal species in Jordan. For Apple hardware

▶ Ijazza Jordan Guide Information on the land and its people, with photos and maps. In both English and Arabic. For Nokia

APPS

▶ www.facebook.com/GOMagJordan?sk=wall Facebook page of the monthly GoMAG Jordan trend magazine

▶ www.7iber.com Independent Jordanian news portal carrying reporting by 'citizen journalists'

▶ www.facebook.com/Jordan Facebook page of trendy JO Magazine with up-to-date news and user commentaries

NETWORKS

TRAVEL TIPS

ARRIVAL

✈ The airlines Royal Jordanian *(www. rj.com)*, bmi *(www.flybmi.com)* and easyJet *(www.easyjet.com)* fly several times a week direct from London to Amman, with a journey time of around five-and-a-half hours, and adding two hours to the London time zone. From New York and Chicago, Jordan is served by US Airways *(www.usairways.com)* and Royal Jordanian *(www.rj.com)*. In Amman travellers arrive at the Queen Alia Airport, 32km/20mi outside the city. Taxis can be hired at the airport. While the fares are fixed, to be on the safe side, get the driver to confirm the price for you. Driving into Amman (45 min.) or Madaba (60 min.) costs approx. 20–25 JD. Here's a tip: many hotels in Amman and Madaba offer a pickup service that is cheaper than the airport taxis. Make early enquiries! In the daytime, an airport express bus runs to the Tabarbur bus station in the north of Amman (every 30–60 min., journey time 60 min., ticket 4 JD). From Tabarbur, a taxi into the city centre only costs around 2–3 JD. If you'd like to get off before the terminal, don't stow your luggage down in the hold, take it with you on the bus. The express bus doesn't always arrive at the airport on time and can be difficult to find sometimes.

🚗 Overland: from Israel via three border crossings – Sheikh Hussein Bridge, King Hussein Bridge (issuing no visas) and Wadi Araba (between Aqaba and Eilat) – or from Syria at the Jaber crossing. From Egypt, you can take a ferry at Sinai.

BANKS & MONEY

Banks are open Sunday through Thursday between 8.30am and 3pm. The cheapest way to change money is in the private bureaux de change. You can use your credit cards (Visa, Mastercard and American Express) at banks and cashpoints to take out money and also to pay in many major shops and hotels.

CAR HIRE

Numerous international car rental firms operate in Jordan, often with branches in the major hotels. Prices hover between 35 and 50 JD/day. The local companies are also usually reliable. While it might be cheaper to book on arrival, bookings made from home tend to be better secured. *Avis tel. 06 5 69 94 20 30 | Dalleh tel. 06 5 511112 | Hertz tel. 06 5 62 41 91 | Sixt tel. 06 5 65 22 07*

CLIMATE, WHEN TO GO

The best time to travel is between March

RESPONSIBLE TRAVEL

It doesn't take a lot to be environmentally friendly whilst travelling. Don't just think about your carbon footprint whilst flying to and from your holiday destination but also about how you can protect nature and culture abroad. As a tourist it is especially important to respect nature, look out for local products, cycle instead of driving, save water and much more. If you would like to find out more about eco-tourism please visit: www.ecotourism.org

From arrival to weather

Holiday from start to finish: the most important addresses and information for your trip to Jordan

and mid-June and then again between September and November. In winter, Amman and the north get some snow, and it is cold and may rain. In the summer months it is stiflingly hot in the south and at the Dead Sea.

CONSULATES & EMBASSIES

UK EMBASSY

Abdoun | Amman 11118 | tel. 06 5 90 92 00 | http://ukinjordan.fco.gov.uk/en/

US EMBASSY

Abdoun, Al-Umawyeen St. | Amman 11118 Jordan | tel. 06 5 90 60 00 | ResponseAmman@state.gov

EMBASSY OF THE HASHEMITE KINGDOM OF JORDAN

6 Upper Phillimore Gardens | London, W8 7HA | tel. 0207 9 37 36 85 | london@fm.gov.jo | www.jordanembassy.org.uk 3504 International Drive, N.W. | Washington, D.C. 20008 | tel. 0202 9 66 26 64 | HKJEmbassyDC@jordanembassyus.org | http://www.jordanembassyus.org

CUSTOMS

Coming into Jordan, you can bring 200 cigarettes or 200g of tobacco, as well as two bottles of wine or one bottle of spirits duty free. There are no restrictions on bringing in foreign currency. Taking archaeological antiquities out of Jordan is prohibited. Duty-free quantities for bringing into the EU include 200 cigarettes or 250g tobacco, 1l of alcohol above 22 vol. and 2l of alcohol up to 22 vol., as well as presents up to the value of 305 £/565 $ (if coming in overland 245 £/395 $). Re-

BUDGETING

Tea	0.25 £ / 0.40 $	
	for a glass in the Old Town	
Falafel	from 0.83 £ / 1.30 $	
	for a falafel sandwich	
Beer	4.50 £ / 7.30 $	
	for a glass (0.3 l) at the hotel	
Shisha pipe	from 10 £ / 16 $	
	as a souvenir in the Old Town	
Taxi	1–2 £ / 1.60–3.30 $	
	city fare	
Newspaper	0.25 £ / 0.40 $	
	for the Jordan Times	

duced allowances apply to children and adolescents up to and including 17 years of age. Cash over 8100 £/13,100 $ has to be officially declared on return to the EU. Travellers entering the USA from Jordan have a duty-free allowance once every 30 days of 800 $ of accompanied baggage, including not more than 200 cigarettes and 100 cigars, and one litre of alcoholic beverages (travellers above the age of 21). For full details, see www.cbp.gov.

DRIVING

Travellers with their own car require an international drivers license and a Carnet de Passage (obtainable from the RAC or AA at home). A third-party damage policy has to be taken out at the border. You have to belt up and mustn't use a mobile phone while driving. Unleaded petrol is not available at all stations. Numerous radar speed checks operate along the motorways (max. speed 110kmh/68mph). Penalties are hefty and payable on the spot!

The network of roads is in good condition and driving a rental car doesn't usually present any problems. Signposting is a different matter. Detours around road works are often not sufficiently marked. Local vehicles are often not monitored the way they should be, so that in the

dark, all of a sudden an unlit truck or a car parked in a dangerous position might materialise alongside the road. Be particularly careful during night drives – try to arrive at your destination before darkness if you can. If you're only planning a short

stay it may be better to rent a car with driver. Depending on distances covered, costs vary between 50 and 100 JD per day, accommodation extra. Chauffeured cars are available from the car rental firms; alternatively ask at the reception of your hotel or directly at a taxi rank.

ELECTRICITY

220 volt, two-pin adapters are required.

EMERGENCY

The central emergency number 911 covers police, fire services, emergency medical assistance and vehicle breakdowns

HEALTH

There is no need for specific vaccinations. Hygiene is usually very good, and medical provision available nearly in every corner of the country. Avoid tap water (mineral water is the best option), as well as salads and fresh fruit if you have a sensitive stomach. Diarrhoea may occasionally occur, but serious diseases are rare. Always travel with toilet paper.

Make sure to take out a good travel health insurance policy. Amman has excellent doctors and hospitals. A recommendation for emergencies is the Arab Center for Heart and Special Surgery *(behind the Sheraton-Hotel | tel. 06 5 92 11 99)*. Treatments have to be paid for in cash.

IMMIGRATION

Your passport has to be valid for at least six months on the day of entering the country. A visa can be issued without problems at Amman airport. The 20 JD have to be paid in Jordanian currency. Next to the visa counter you'll find a bank for changing money. The visa re-

CURRENCY CONVERTER

£	JD	JD	£
1	1.10	1	0.90
3	3.30	3	2.70
5	5.50	5	4.50
13	14.30	13	11.70
40	44	40	36
75	82.50	75	67.50
120	132	120	108
250	275	250	225
500	550	500	450

$	JD	JD	$
1	0.70	1	1.40
3	2.10	3	4.20
5	3.50	5	7
13	9.10	13	18.20
40	28	40	56
75	52.50	75	105
120	84	120	168
250	175	250	350
500	350	500	700

For current exchange rates see www.xe.com

mains valid for four weeks and may be extended at any police station.

A multi-entry visa has to be requested before starting your trip from the Jordanian embassy (see Consulates & Embassies) and costs 50 £/80 $. One thing to look out for if entering via Aqaba: the visa is free and valid for a whole month for the entire country. However, it can only be extended in Aqaba. Due to the volatile political situation in the West Bank, independent travellers should use the Sheikh Hussein checkpoint in the north for crossing the Jordanian-Israeli border for a quick visit to Jerusalem. If planning to travel back into Jordan from Israel, organise a multi-entry visa for Jordan beforehand.

INFORMATION

JORDAN TOURISM BOARD

– *The Brighter Group Limited / Jordan Tourism Board | London's Vertical Gateway | Bridges Court Road | London SW11 3BE | tel. 020 72 23 18 78 | UK@visitjordan.com| www.visitjordan.com*

– *JTB North America / 1307 Dolley Madison Blvd., Suite 2A | McLean, VA 22101 | tel. 01 703 243 7404/5 | contactus@visitjordan.com| www.visitjordan.com*

– *Tunis Street | Amman | between 4th and 5th Circle, next to the duty-free shop | tel. 06 5 67 82 94 | www.visitjordan.com*

Nearly every place of any tourist significance now has a state-run visitor centre. These are usually open all day long (except during Ramadan) and offer tickets, information, guided tours and basic services such as toilets and first aid. In places without visitor centres, the tourist police can help. The helpful agents usually speak English.

MEDIA

In most hotels you can receive satellite programmes. The second Jordanian TV channel broadcasts in English and French. Radio Jordan too broadcasts on FM 96.3 MHz in English, BBC World on MW 103.1 MHz. The English-language Jordan Times daily newspaper appears Sundays to Fridays. The English-language lifestyle magazine JO! is published monthly. Another option is to subscribe to the Jordanian news agency, Petra, as an English-language RSS feed.

OPENING HOURS

Jordanian authorities and banks are closed on Fridays and Saturdays, many private companies only on Fridays, some Christian shops also on Sundays. Some shops are open on Friday afternoons, and supermarkets (Safeway, Cosmo) remain open around the clock.

PERSONAL SAFETY

Currently many states in the Arab world are experiencing protest movements demanding political change from their governments. In Jordan too there have been demonstrations in various cities. Travellers are strongly advised to avoid large gatherings and demonstrations, not to take photographs of them and to exercise special caution. Carefully follow reports in the media and check the up-to-date advice on the embassies' websites.

PHONE & MOBILE PHONE

If you want to keep using your home mobile phone, get hold of a tourist SIM card offered by the Jordan company Zain ('Zain Visitors'). At a cost of 6 JD, it is valid for three months, rechargeable but not extendable. Important: your mobile must be unlocked. Zain also offers prepaid packages for the iphone 4 as well as for mobile internet (www.jo.zain.com/english).

Country code Jordan: 00962. Calling from abroad and/or with a foreign mobile phone, leave out the zero of the local code or mobile number (e.g. 0-79).

To call a Jordanian mobile from a Jordanian landline, dial the network code with the zero (e.g. 079 or 077). To call abroad from Jordan, dial 0044 (UK), 00353 (ROI) or 001 (USA/Canada). National directory enquiries are provided by Jordan Telecom (Orange) tel. 121, (English/Arabic). The number for directory enquiries can change at short notice. If in doubt check the Jordan Times under 'Directory Assistance/Enquiries'.

PHOTOGRAPHY

You can take pictures of everything apart from military installations and the palaces of the Royal Family. If you would like to photograph people, request permission first.

POST

A postcard takes between 4 and 6 days to reach Europe (800 fils), longer to North America, a parcel (max. 20 kg, around 45 JD for 10 kg) approx. 8–10 days. www.jordanpost.com.jo

PRICES & CURRENCY

The Jordanian dinar (in common parlance jaydee, after the abbreviation JD) is divided into 100 piastres or 1000 fils. Prices are often given in fils, so don't be alarmed if a pack of cigarettes costs 800 fils: that's equivalent to 0.80 JD. The dinar is pegged to the US dollar.

WEATHER IN AMMAN

	Jan	Feb	March	April	May	June	July	Aug	Sept	Oct	Nov	Dec
Daytime temperatures in °C/°F	13/55	14/57	17/63	23/73	28/82	31/88	32/90	33/91	31/88	28/82	21/70	15/59
Nighttime temperatures in °C/°F	4/40	5/41	7/45	10/50	15/59	17/63	19/66	19/66	18/64	14/57	10/50	6/43
Sunshine hours/day	6	8	10	10	11	14	14	13	12	10	8	6
Precipitation days/month	8	8	4	3	1	0	0	0	0	1	4	5

PUBLIC TRANSPORT

Travellers wanting to take a minibus from Amman to other towns and cities have to first get themselves to the central Tabarbur bus station (taxi from the city centre approx. 2.50 JD | minibuses 1–5 JD depending on distance). The bus companies JETT *(www.jett.com.jo)* and Trust operate connections into all larger towns and cities several times a day, some of them in several categories (e.g. JETT Amman–Aqaba: 8 JD (normal), 17 JD (luxury). Between Petra and Aqaba there is only a taxi service. Watch out: on Fridays and Saturdays many routes have fewer buses. Book in good time and find out departure times in advance!

The only domestic flight route is Amman–Aqaba. There are two daily flights from Marka airport in the east of town (one-way 50 min, 50 JD).

The country's only railway route is the Hejaz railway *(information tel. 06 4 89 54 13)*, which was built by the Ottomans in the early 20th century. Twice a week a train runs between Amman and Damascus (approx. 200km/125mi, around 8 hrs.).

SWIMMING & BEACHES

Plenty of sun, crystal-clear waters and stunning coral reefs – Jordan is just made for a holiday spent swimming and diving. However, the lack of long coastlines and the conservative mentality of the population mean that undisturbed public places for free swimming and sunbathing are rare. For a handful of dinars more you'll easily find alternatives. Private beaches on the Dead Sea, with pool, shower and changing facilities cost 10–15 JD/day. While hotel beaches are significantly more expensive, the entrance fee usually comprises a food or drink voucher (see Dead Sea chapter). In Aqaba, diving clubs and smaller hotels offer access to pools/private beaches, partly incl. sun lounger, sunshade and towel from as little as 8 JD/day. In major hotels in the centre und in Tala Bay, fees for pool and beach use start at 30 JD/day incl. lunch/drink.

TAXI

In Jordan's larger cities, taxis are the most popular way to get around. White shared taxis ('serviis') ply fixed routes (between 7am and 7pm). Yellow taxis have no fixed rank, so just flag them down off the street, but do insist that the driver switches on the taximeter. These days, Amman also has radio cabs that you can order by phone to a particular address, e.g. *Al Moumayyaz, tel. 06 5 79 99 99, www.taxi-jo.com*

TIME

In both winter and summer, Jordan is ahead of Greenwich Mean Time by two hours.

TIPPING

Restaurants add 10 per cent to the bill, but a small gratuity for waiters and maids is recommended. Porters usually receive half a dinar, and taxi fares are rounded up by around 300 fils.

WHAT TO WEAR

Between April and October lightweight cotton clothing and a jumper for cool nights are sufficient. A sun hat is obligatory. In winter you'll need warm clothing for Amman and the north, while the Dead Sea and Aqaba still enjoy spring temperatures. Make sure to bring sturdy ankle-height shoes for hikes and visiting Petra.

NOTES

MARCO POLO TRAVEL GUIDES

ALGARVE
AMSTERDAM
AUSTRALIA
BANGKOK
BARCELONA
BERLIN
BRUSSELS
BUDAPEST
CALIFORNIA
CAPE TOWN
  WINE LANDS,
  GARDEN ROUTE
COLOGNE
CORFU
GRAN CANARIA
CRETE
CUBA
CYPRUS
  NORTH AND SOUTH
DUBAI

DUBROVNIK &
  DALMATIAN COAST
EDINBURGH
EGYPT
FINLAND
FLORENCE
FLORIDA
FRENCH RIVIERA
  NICE, CANNES &
  MONACO
HONGKONG
  MACAU
IRELAND
ISRAEL
ISTANBUL
JORDAN
KOS

LAKE GARDA
LANZAROTE
LAS VEGAS
LONDON
LOS ANGELES
MADEIRA
  PORTO SANTO
MALLORCA
MALTA
  GOZO
MOROCCO
NEW YORK
NEW ZEALAND
NORWAY
PARIS
RHODES

ROME
SAN FRANCISCO
SICILY
SOUTH AFRICA
STOCKHOLM
TENERIFE
THAILAND
TURKEY
  SOUTH COAST
UNITED ARAB
  EMIRATES
VENICE
VIETNAM

- PACKED WITH INSIDER TIPS
- BEST WALKS AND TOURS
- FULL-COLOUR PULL-OUT MAP
  AND STREET ATLAS

ROAD ATLAS

The green line ▬▬ indicates the Trips & Tours (p. 86–91)
The blue line ▬▬ indicates the Perfect route (p. 30–31)

All tours are also marked on the pull-out map

Photo: Street of columns in Jerash

Exploring Jordan

The map on the back cover shows how the area has been sub-divided

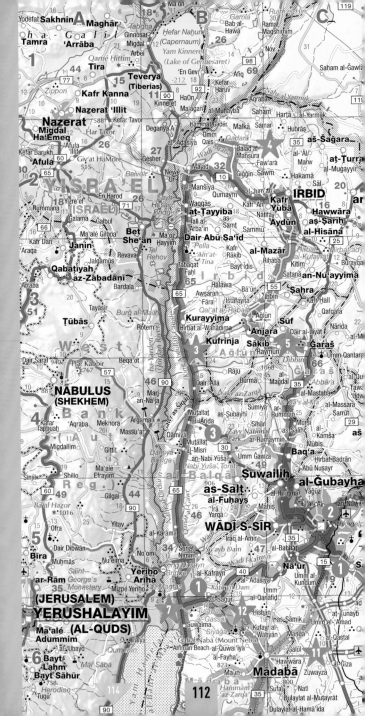

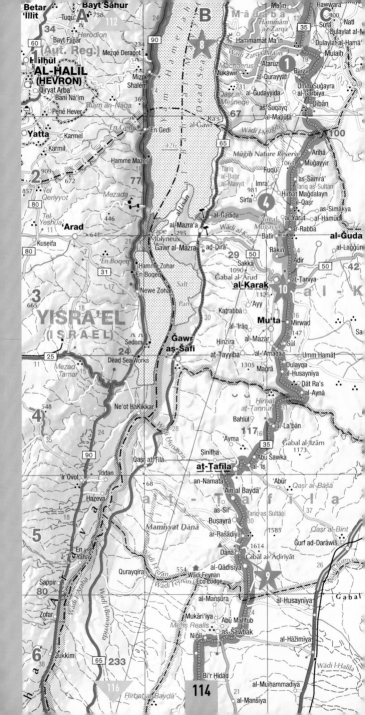

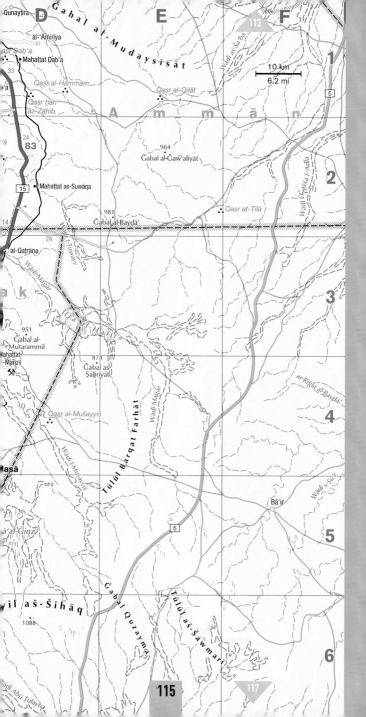

Qunaytira

D   E   F

Ǧabal al-Mudaysīsāt

al-'Āmirīya

Qaṣr Dab'a
Maḥaṭṭat Dab'a

33

Qaṣr al-Ḥammām

Qaṣr al-Qilāt

Qaṣr han
az-Ẓahib

A   m   m   ā   n

24
83

964
Ǧabal al-Ǧaw'aliyāt

Maḥaṭṭat as-Suwāqa

15

981
Ǧabal al-Bayḍā'

Qaṣr aṭ-Ṭīlā

14
al-Qaṭrāna

24

Ḥuwayy

Wādī Maǧar

a   **k**

951
Ǧabal al-
Mutarammil
Maḥaṭṭat
-Manzil

874
Ǧabal aš-Ṣaḥrīyāt

ar-Riǧla al-Bayḍā'

Qaṣr al-Mušayyiš

Wādī Maǧar

Wādī Mušayyiš

Tūlūl Barqat Farḥāt

Maṣā

Bā'ir

Wādī s-Sūr

5

5

ā al-Ǧinz

vil aš-Šiḥāq

Ǧabal Quzaymā

Tūlūl aš-Šawmari

1088

Wādī Abū Tulayḥa

10 km
6.2 mi

Wādī aš-Šaba

Wādī Ġwēṣa l-Adla

1

2

3

4

5

6

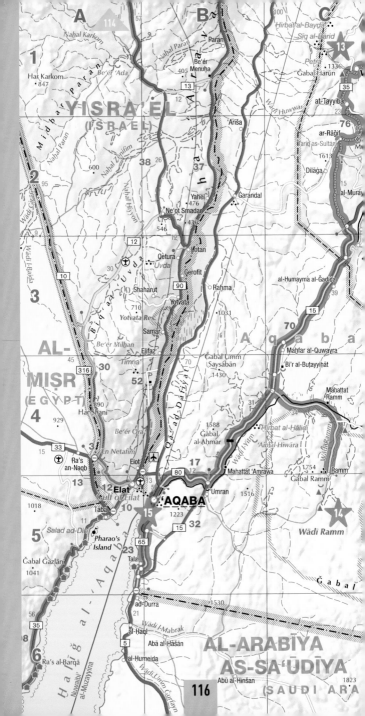

A B C

1 Nahal Karkom
57
100
Hirbat al-Bayḍa
Sīq al-Barid
13
Petra
Ĝabal Hārūn 1336
Be'ér 'Ada
Har Karkom
847
405
Be'ér Menuha
13
at-Tayyiba
Wadi Huwwar
23
76
ar-Rāĝif
Ṭariq as-Sulṭāni
YISRA'EL
(ISRAEL)
Arīša
2
Nahal Ḥiyyon
600
38 26
37
Garandal
Dilāğa
1613
al-Mura
Nahal Zniifim
Yahel 476
Ne'ot Smadar
430
546
al-Humaymā al-Ĝadida
Qèṭura
12
Uvda
Gerofit
39
3
K) Shaharut
710
90
Rahma
15
Yotvata
70
Yotvata Res.
Be'er Milhan
Samar
1031
A q a b a
Elifaz
Ĝabal Umm
Timna
Saysābān
Bi'r al-Buṭayyihāt
AL-
45
1430
Mahattat
MIṢR
316
30
52
Ramm
(EGYPT)
890
Har Shani
31
4
929
Be'ér Ora
1588
Ĝabal
al-Aḥmar
Hirbat al-Ḫālidi
Ain al-Ḥiwāra
En Netafim
13
31
Ra's
an-Naqb
17
Mahaṭṭat 'Amrawa
1754
Ramm
12
80
Ĝabal Ramm
13
12 Elat
Elot
Umran
1516
'AQABA
1223
10
15
Tābā
15
32
5 Salad ad-Diḡ
Pharao's
Island
23
14
Ĝabal Ġazlān
65
Wādi Ramm
1041
Tala
ad-Durra
1530
21
56
35
al-Ḥaql
Wādi l-Mabrak
8
5
AL-'ARABĪYA
6
Ra's al-Barqā
al-Ḥumeida
Abā al-Ḥāšān
AS-SA'ŪDĪYA
1823
Abū al-Hinšān
(SAUDI ARA
116

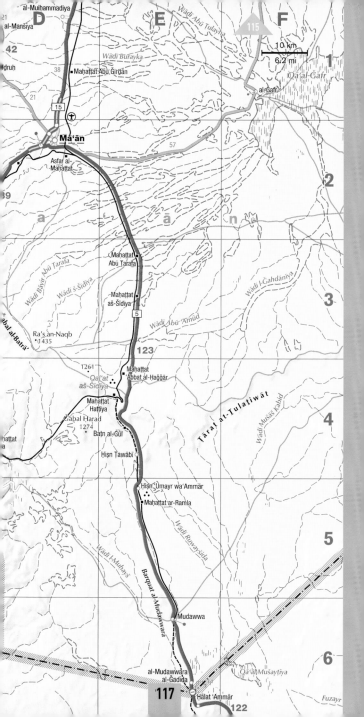

al-Muhammadiya
al-Mansiya

D

E

Wādī Abū Tulayha

115

F

42

druh

38

Mahaṭṭat Abū Ǧirǧān

Qaʿal-Ǧafr

1

21

10 km

6.2 mi

al-Ǧafr

15

Maʿān

57

2

Asfar al-
Mahaṭṭat

39

ā

n

a

Wādī Bāṭin Abū Ṭarafa

Wādī š-Šidīya

Mahaṭṭat
Abū Ṭarafa

Wādī l-Ǧahdānīya

3

Mahaṭṭat
aš-Šidīya

5

Wādī Abū ʿAmūd

Ra's an-Naqb
△ 435

Gabal al-Batrā'

123

1261

Qalʿat
aš-Šidīya

Mahaṭṭat
ʿAbbat al-Haǧǧār

Wādī Mušāš Kabīd

Mahaṭṭat
Hattiya

Gabal Harad
1274

Batn al-Ǧūl

Tārat al-Tulatiwāt

4

Hisṇ Ṭawābi

Hisṇ ʿUmayr wa ʿAmmār

Mahaṭṭat ar-Ramla

Wādī Ruwayšida

5

Wādī l-Mu ḥayṣ

Barquat al-Mudawwara

Mudawwa

Qaʿ al-Mušaytīya

6

al-Mudawwāra
al-Ǧadīda

Hālat ʿAmmār

117

122

Fuzayr

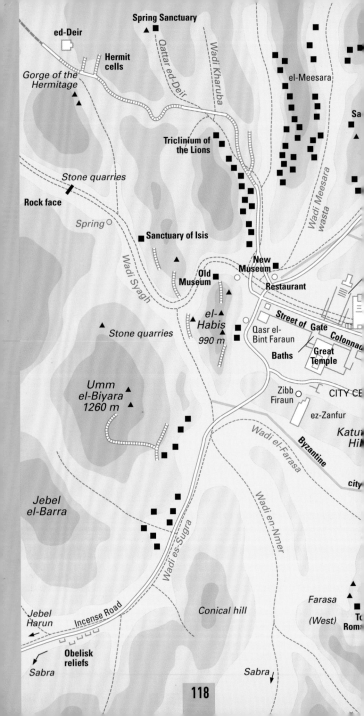

ed-Deir

Spring Sanctuary

Hermit cells

Gorge of the Hermitage

Qattar ed-Deir

Wadi Kharuba

el-Meesara

Sa

Triclinium of the Lions

Stone quarries

Rock face

Spring

Sanctuary of Isis

New Museum

Wadi Syagh

Old Museum

Restaurant

el-Habis
990 m

Street of Gate

Colonnad

Qasr el-Bint Faraun

Baths

Great Temple

Stone quarries

Umm el-Biyara
1260 m

Zibb Firaun

CITY CE

ez-Zanfur

Wadi el-Farasa

Byzantine

Katu
Hil

city

Jebel el-Barra

Wadi es-Sugra

Wadi en-Nmer

Jebel Harun

Incense Road

Obelisk reliefs

Conical hill

Farasa

(West)

To
Rom

Sabra

Sabra

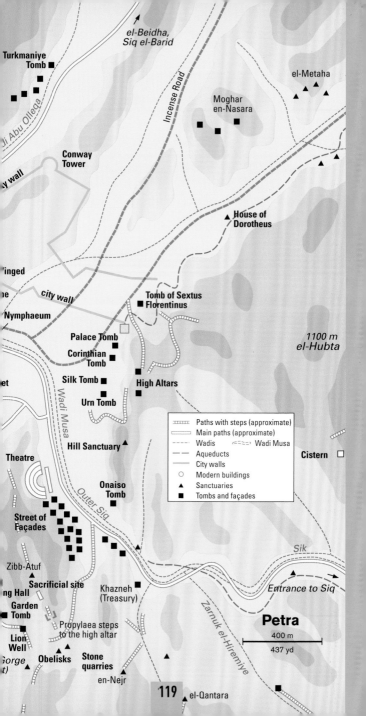

el-Beidha,
Siq el-Barid

**Turkmaniye
Tomb** ■

■ ■ ■

■

Wadi Abu Olleqa

Incense Road

el-Metaha
▲ ▲ ▲ ▲

Moghar
en-Nasara
■
■

**Conway
Tower**

▲

▲ House of
Dorotheus

'inged
e
Nymphaeum

city wall

**Tomb of Sextus
Florentinus**
■

1100 m
el-Hubta

Palace Tomb ■

**Corinthian
Tomb** ■

■

Silk Tomb ■

■ **High Altars**
■

Urn Tomb ■

Hill Sanctuary ▲

Wadi Musa

Theatre

**Onaiso
Tomb** ■

Outer Siq

□ **Cistern**

et

**Street of
Façades**
■ ■
■ ■ ■
■ ■
■ ■
■ ■

▲

Sik

▲
Entrance to Siq →

Zibb-Atuf
Sacrificial site

ng Hall

**Garden
Tomb**
■

**Lion
Well**

Gorge
t)

Obelisks

**Khazneh
(Treasury)** ■

▲

Propylaea steps
to the high altar

**Stone
quarries**
en-Nejr

Zarnuk el-Hiremiye

▲

Petra

400 m
―――――――
437 yd

⊥⊥⊥⊥	Paths with steps (approximate)
▭▭▭	Main paths (approximate)
- - -	Wadis ⸗⸗⸗ Wadi Musa
— —	Aqueducts
——	City walls
○	Modern buildings
▲	Sanctuaries
■	Tombs and façades

119 ▲ el-Qantara

KEY TO ROAD ATLAS

—18—26— Autobahn mit Anschlussstellen
Motorway with junctions

======= Autobahn in Bau
Motorway under construction

I Mautstelle
Toll station

O Raststätte mit Übernachtung
Roadside restaurant and hotel

⊛ Raststätte
Roadside restaurant

⊛ Tankstelle
Filling-station

——— Autobahnähnliche Schnell-
straße mit Anschlussstelle
Dual carriage-way with
motorway characteristics
with junction

——— Fernverkehrsstraße
Trunk road

——— Durchgangsstraße
Thoroughfare

——— Wichtige Hauptstraße
Important main road

——— Hauptstraße
Main road

——— Nebenstraße
Secondary road

——— Eisenbahn
Railway

🚗 Autozug-Terminal
Car-loading terminal

········· Zahnradbahn
Mountain railway

I-o-o-o-o-I Kabinenschwebebahn
Aerial cableway

·········· Eisenbahnfähre
Railway ferry

—🚗— Autofähre
Car ferry

--------- Schifffahrtslinie
Shipping route

——— Landschaftlich besonders
schöne Strecke
Route with
beautiful scenery

Alleenstr. Touristenstraße
Tourist route

XI-V Wintersperre
Closure in winter

× × × × × Straße für Kfz gesperrt
Road closed to motor traffic

8% Bedeutende Steigungen
Important gradients

🚐 Für Wohnwagen nicht
empfehlenswert
Not recommended
for caravans

🚐 Für Wohnwagen gesperrt
Closed for caravans

☼ Besonders schöner Ausblick
Important panoramic view

* *Wartenstein*
* *Umbalfälle* Sehenswert: Kultur - Natur
Of interest: culture - nature

Badestrand
Bathing beach

Nationalpark, Naturpark
National park, nature park

Sperrgebiet
Prohibited area

⋮ Kirche
Church

⋔ Kloster
Monastery

⋮ Schloss, Burg
Palace, castle

⋎ Moschee
Mosque

⋮ ⋮ ⋮ ⋮ Ruinen
Ruins

⚐ Leuchtturm
Lighthouse

⋮ Turm
Tower

∩ Höhle
Cave

∴ Ausgrabungsstätte
Archaeological excavation

▲ Jugendherberge
Youth hostel

♠ Allein stehendes Hotel
Isolated hotel

⌂ Berghütte
Refuge

▲ Campingplatz
Camping site

✈ Flughafen
Airport

✈ Regionalflughafen
Regional airport

✈ Flugplatz
Airfield

·—·—·—· Staatsgrenze
National boundary

------ Verwaltungsgrenze
Administrative boundary

⊖ Grenzkontrollstelle
Check-point

⊖ Grenzkontrollstelle mit
Beschränkung
Check-point with
restrictions

ROMA Hauptstadt
Capital

VENÉZIA Verwaltungssitz
Seat of the administration

Ausflüge & Touren
Trips & Tours

Perfekte Route
Perfect route

★1 MARCO POLO Highlight
MARCO POLO Highlight

INDEX

This index lists all places, destinations and important personalities mentioned in the guide, as well as a few other concepts. Page numbers in bold type refer to the main entry.

WRITE TO US

e-mail: info@marcopologuides.co.uk

Did you have a great holiday? Is there something on your mind? Whatever it is, let us know! Whether you want to praise, alert us to errors or give us a personal tip – MARCO POLO would be pleased to hear from you. We do everything we can to provide the very latest information for your trip.

Nevertheless, despite all of our authors' thorough research, errors can creep in. MARCO POLO does not accept any liability for this. Please contact us by e-mail or post.

MARCO POLO Travel Publishing Ltd
Pinewood, Chineham Business Park
Crockford Lane, Chineham
Basingstoke, Hampshire RG24 8AL
United Kingdom

PICTURE CREDITS
Cover photograph: camels in Wadi Rum (Laif/hemis.fr: Mattes)
Images: @fotolia.com: erwinova (16 bottom); Darna Village (17 bottom); DuMont Bildarchiv: Gartung (52, 99); Huber: Borchi (44), Simeone (114/115), Ripani (27, 102 bottom), Szyszka (15); F. Ihlow (6, 88); centre Kirchgessner (flap r., 3 centre, 4, 8, 22, 26 l., 28/29, 29, 30 l., 30 r., 34, 46, 48, 55, 58, 61, 62, 64/65, 83, 86/87, 95, 97, 98/99, 103); Laif/hemis.fr: Giuglio (91), Mattes (1 top), Laif: Eid (flap l., 2 centre, 2 centre bottom, 42/43, 80/81), Gaasterland (3 top, 28, 56/57), Gumm (2 centre top, 18/19, 32/33, 37), Hemispheres (24/25), Heuer (72, 74, 85), Riehle (40); Rima Malallah (16 top); mauritius images: age (20), Bibikow (39, 68, 96/97), CuboImages (12/13, 66); mauritius images/imagebroker: de Cuveland (9), Eisele-Hein (2 top, 5), von Poser (26 r.); H. Mielke (2 bottom, 3 bottom, 7, 10/11, 50/51, 70, 76/77, 78, 96, 102 top); centre Sabra (1 bottom); T. Stankiewicz (98); The Royal Society for the Conservation of Nature (17 top); Terhaal Eco Adventure: Rakan Mehyar (16 centre); vario images: imagebroker (92/93)

1st Edition 2013
Worldwide Distribution: Marco Polo Travel Publishing Ltd, Pinewood, Chineham Business Park, Crockford Lane, Basingstoke, Hampshire RG24 8AL, United Kingdom. Email: sales@marcopolouk.com
© MAIRDUMONT GmbH & Co. KG, Ostfildern
Chief editors: Michaela Lienemann (concept, managing editor), Marion Zorn (concept, text editor)
Author: Andrea Nüsse; co-author: Martina Sabra; editor: Cordula Natusch
Programme supervision: Anita Dahlinger, Ann-Katrin Kutzner, Nikolai Michaelis
Picture editor: Gabriele Forst, Iris Kaczmarczyk
What's hot: wunder media, Munich;
Cartography road: © MAIRDUMONT, Ostfildern; Cartography pull-out map: © MAIRDUMONT, Ostfildern
Design: milchhof : atelier, Berlin; Front cover, pull-out map cover, page 1: factor product munich
Translated from German by Kathleen Becker, Lisbon; editor of the English edition: John Sykes, Cologne
Prepress: BW-Medien GmbH, Leonberg

DOS & DON'TS ✋

A few things you should look out for while travelling in Jordan

WEARING MINI SKIRTS OR SHORTS

Jordanians are polite and will not pester you for wearing revealing clothing. However, if you want to appear less of a tourist and connect with the local population, proper clothing is the recommended option: long trousers for men and skirts or trousers that cover the knee for women. Even in the most boiling heat you won't see a single Jordanian wearing shorts, except amongst the upper-class youth in Amman. Things are different at tourist sites such as the beaches of Aqaba, Wadi Rum or during hiking tours: here short trousers are not a problem. For mosque visits women should always carry a headscarf.

TOUCHING CORALS OR FISH

It is not only for conservation's sake that you shouldn't touch anything while diving or snorkelling. The underwater world of the Red Sea features fish and corals that are exceedingly toxic. The spikes of sea urchins also break off easily and remain stuck under the skin. Breaking off corals is a criminal offence, so look but don't touch!

REVEALING YOUR ATHEISM

By all means take opportunities for interesting discussions about religion and Islam. Avoid presenting yourself as an atheist, though, as you will only earn surprised incomprehension, and your revelation might put an end to the conversation. In the Arab world there are very few – if any – intellectuals who profess to have no God. Atheism is frowned upon and not socially acceptable. Jews and Christians however are accepted and respected as 'People of the Book' (Torah, Bible).

UNDERESTIMATING THE HEAT AND COLD

Jordan has extreme differences in temperature. If you are travelling in Wadi Rum or Aqaba in summer, always carry water bottles and a hat, as temperatures here rise above 40°C/104°F. However, in Amman, which lies at an altitude of nearly 1000m/3300ft, you'll often need a light jumper even on summer nights. If you're travelling to Jordan in winter, dress up warm. Not only does Amman and the north of the country get regular snow – even if only for a short time, a night in the desert can be freezing cold in late October already. Make sure to pack a down jacket and warm underwear.

FORGETTING YOUR ID

Always carry your passport with you, particularly if visiting the Dead Sea, the Jordan Valley and Aqaba, etc. Without documents you will be turned back at any of the numerous checkpoints.